Liberating Mindfulness

T0243363

Liberating Mindfulness

FROM BILLION-DOLLAR INDUSTRY TO ENGAGED SPIRITUALITY

Gail J. Stearns

ORBIS BOOKS
Maryknoll, New York

Founded in 1970, Orbis Books endeavors to publish works that enlighten the mind, nourish the spirit, and challenge the conscience. The publishing arm of the Maryknoll Fathers and Brothers, Orbis seeks to explore the global dimensions of the Christian faith and mission, to invite dialogue with diverse cultures and religious traditions, and to serve the cause of reconciliation and peace. The books published reflect the views of their authors and do not represent the official position of the Maryknoll Society. To learn more about Orbis Books, please visit our website at www.orbisbooks.com.

Copyright © 2022 by Gail J. Stearns.

Published by Orbis Books, Box 302, Maryknoll, NY 10545–0302.

Manufactured in the United States of America

Library of Congress Cataloging-in-Publication Data

Names: Stearns, Gail J., 1956- author.
Title: Liberating mindfulness : from billion-dollar industry to engaged
    spirituality / Gail J. Stearns.
Description: Maryknoll, NY : Orbis Books, [2022] | Includes bibliographical
    references and index. | Summary: "Attempts to reclaim mindfulness from
    the commercial and corporate juggernaut it has become and to demonstrate
    its usefulness in spiritual (including Christian) life"-- Provided by
    publisher.
Identifiers: LCCN 2021049881 (print) | LCCN 2021049882 (ebook) | ISBN
    9781626984714 (trade paperback) | ISBN 9781608339334 (epub)
Subjects: LCSH: Christianity--Psychology. | Mindfulness (Psychology) |
    Thought and thinking--Religious aspects. | Attention. | Awareness. |
    Psychology, Religious. | Spiritual life.
Classification: LCC BR110 .S718 2022 (print) | LCC BR110 (ebook) | DDC
    261.5/15--dc23/eng/20211115
LC record available at https://lccn.loc.gov/2021049881
LC ebook record available at https://lccn.loc.gov/2021049882

This book is dedicated to the memory of five people.

*To Mom, whose life and spirit is woven
into my life and into these pages.*

*And to four persons who were
natural contemplatives and persons of deep faith.*

To Ron and Dad for being the ground beneath my feet.

To my brother-in-law, Steve.

To Sharon, my spiritual companion on the journey.

I carry each of you in my heart.

*To
Ron Richard
Steve Upmeyer
Sharon Kehoe
Ben and Mary Stearns*

Contents

Acknowledgments

The journey of writing this book has been one of puzzlement and wonder. I questioned many concepts, such as mindfulness and happiness, that I once took for granted as needing no explanation. One of those concepts is gratitude. So to begin with my deep gratitude for the village of persons who allowed me the time and resources to write and to simply "be" throughout these past few years is humbling. In these pages, I discuss gratitude as involving both resistance to individualism limited to "my" blessings as though someone owed me, as well as including thanks for abundance of all of life. It is in the spirit of resistance and abundance that I thank so many whom I see as partners in the work of resisting co-opted understandings of mindfulness and its uses and celebrating the abundance it may offer as we awaken to new vision.

Those who read drafts and gave me honest opinions helped to bring more heart to the book: my son, John Moody, and dear friends Susanna Branch and Jody Theissan. Julie Artman, whom I respect greatly as my peer in mindfulness teaching, and my sister Nancy Martin, were deeply generous in offering their critiques and editing skills.

I owe much gratitude to my colleagues at the Fish Interfaith Center at Chapman University. You contribute to an amazing team committed to serving our students. Special thanks to Jen Ruby for her steady management and unfailing support as I traveled and wrote to bring these ideas to fruition. I thank Provost Glenn Pfeiffer and faculty at Chapman University who were responsible for granting me a six-month sabbatical leave and awarding me a Faculty Opportunity Fund grant to pursue travel for research. Thank you, Lisa Leitz and David Default, for your friendship and travel help!

I am humbly appreciative of editor Jill Brennan O'Brien for her guidance offered with such great kindness and skill, and deeply grateful to Orbis Books for taking on this project.

I offer a bow of gratitude to those mindfulness and meditation teachers I have sat in retreats with and whose wisdom has expanded my practice and teaching, including Trudy Goodman, Michele McDonald, Jesse Maceo Vega-Frey, Diana Winston, and Mary Grace Orr.

I am so grateful to every person who graced me with time to sit through interviews and allowed me to tell their stories in this book! Ongoing correspondence with many persons helped to sharpen my understanding and writing—you are each named in these pages. To new colleagues I met during the course of traveling and writing, and to long-time friends and former students with whom it was a complete joy to connect—your stories and teachings form the heart of this book. For her generous expertise I thank Cynthia Bourgeault, and for particularly meaningful conversations and friendship, I thank Jim Burklo, Melvin Escobar, and Ben Keckler. Thank you to John Philip Newell and Omid Safi, who were superb guides for experiences of learning about Celtic spirituality and Sufism. Special thanks to former students Sophia Barr, Justice Crudup, and Clairre Kirkpatrick for your openness and continued connection and for the wisdom you shared with me. I am grateful to the many students, faculty, and staff who have taken courses in mindfulness I have offered, who have been so open and have taught me so much.

My family and close friends have been my greatest support through these past several years of grieving, joy, writing, travel, activism, and living through a pandemic. I have been blessed with several spiritual guides and am particularly grateful to Karen Sindelar for opening up my awareness. My gratitude and love to my friends Carol Hoeksema, Beth Shields, and Carolea Webb, and to my cousin Nancy Phillips, who are all ever-present even at a distance.

There are no words to express my thanks to Jane Upmeyer and Nancy Martin for being the best sisters a person could ask for.

Finally, I offer my love to my adult children, John and Jeana Stearns Moody, with thanks for always encouraging me to follow the path of my heart, and for your wisdom, creativity, and inspiration as you each follow yours.

Introduction

The real challenge, one that the mindfulness movement is impaled on, is how do you take the next step from the superficial identity to the deeper identity?[1]

How do we take the next step into greater depth as spiritual beings? And further, how do we take the leap into greater depth communally, toward a just society? You may consider yourself secular, spiritual, or religious. You may have dabbled in mindfulness or attended religious prayers or services. Yet, you may still feel your search has not quite been fulfilling—reaching outward, yet leaving you wondering if deeper inner groundedness is possible.

I teach religious studies, and often ask university students to define spirituality. They reply, almost inevitably, that spirituality is different from religion. It is personal and individual, they say; it is "my own unique path." Religion, in contrast, they tell me, is believing what a group believes. Most of them would describe themselves as more "spiritual" than "religious." I gently suggest to them that spirituality may be the opposite of personal and individual. And that if one is to discover the depths of spirituality, one will discover they are not an individual at all—in fact, they are deeply connected with all of life.

In a similar manner, when I ask students to discuss the purpose of mindfulness practices, which they are all by now familiar with at least in name, they say that these are also individual practices that help them foster better stress regulation. Indeed, mindfulness is largely marketed and taught as a personal stress-relief practice. It is

---

1. Cynthia Bourgeault, interview by author, November 27, 2019.

then suggested that if we all would just do it, it would lessen all our stresses and somehow emanate greater peace and create a more compassionate world. Yet, with my students, I investigate whether it may be doing precisely the opposite: emanating individualist, patriarchal, gendered, and racist social control cleverly disguised as a contemporary, popular promotion. We also investigate a central question of this book: Are we being mindful about mindfulness?

I have been traversing a spiritual journey for many years, through religious engagement to popular, secular mindfulness. In fact, without abandoning beliefs that had grown and matured, I had high hopes that mindfulness offered a new path that would supersede all others. I hoped it would bring depth into my life and others, whether they consider themselves secular, spiritual, or religious. Initially, mindfulness changed my life. It transformed my personal practice of meditation. It enabled me to help other people awaken to self-awareness better than anything else I had previously studied.

Mindfulness is often defined as living in the present with curiosity and without judgment. Most of us can recall mindful moments when we were immersed and curious. Time and space stood still, and we forgot what was before or was to come. These were not just experiences of distraction (like watching TV), but of being fully in the present moment. I recall sitting at the kitchen table with Pauline Thompson, a wise elder whom I interviewed for my first book. As I spoke with her, to my astonishment, I would glance at my watch to discover not one, but five hours had passed as I was enrapt in the rich space woven with story and meaning between us.[2] You may have had such experiences—perhaps while hiking in nature, singing with a choir, or deep in conversation, when time seemed to stand still. You were not anxious at all, but completely present. Mindfulness practices can help lessen our distractedness and be more present in our lives.

---

2. Gail J. Stearns, *Writing Pauline: Wisdom from a Long Life* (Lanham, MD: Hamilton Books, 2005).

If mindfulness transformed my practice, prior to my discovery of it, Christianity grounded my life. Throughout my childhood, on Sunday morning my parents would rise early to prepare various dishes for Sunday dinner before we would head off to church. When we returned home, arriving shortly after us would be the choir director and her family, as well as friends from church, who were my local family growing up. Life centered around food and friends and faith. In this environment, I learned about caring for others as a foundational ethic in my life. I saw in my parents the ethic of doing unto others as you would have them do unto you, and to love your neighbor as yourself, and it was ingrained in me as well. I continued with the Presbyterian Church—graduating from seminary and pastoring a church as an ordained minister. Soon, though, I was hungry to study again, and went back to school for a PhD that intertwined critical gender theory with theology. I have since straddled the spheres of academics and ministry, and this book emerges from the space between the worlds of critical theory and of theological wonder.

I ran a campus ministry and taught university courses, with ample opportunity to engage daily with young adults at the university level. I searched for ways they might discover self-awareness, raise their conscience to the needs of the world around them, and deepen their spirituality. I discovered mindfulness to be the best tool for personal awareness, but for consciousness raising, developing compassion, and spiritual grounding, it fell short. In time, my eyes opened to see that what one does with mindful awareness is deeply dependent on the ethics one already holds and the intention one carries into mindfulness practices. And whether it is a tool for spiritual grounding depends on how deeply one engages in practice with devotion.

Mindfulness emerged into a multi-billion-dollar industry in the years I've been practicing and teaching, through the early decades of this century. Google searches for the term *mindfulness* turn up increasing numbers of results every day—I recently got 235 million in a search of fifty seconds. In recent years I have found myself increasingly disillusioned with the ethics underlying much of this mindfulness profit-chasing movement around me. I began to suspect that dependent on the social context and understanding of persons in society, a transformative tool such as mindfulness can be used powerfully for good or for lethal means, for ushering in liberation or for tightening complicity.

Uncovering Contemplative Practices

Granted a six-month study leave from my university, I set out to study the mindfulness movement to discover its potential and its dangers. As I investigated mindfulness, I found myself gravitating toward ancient wisdom traditions. I uncovered in new ways this surprising discovery: that something like mindfulness continues to be practiced in many of these, even within my own tradition of Christianity.

I realized quickly I would get nowhere in my search unless I approached this time critically, but also mindfully and spiritually. I embarked on what I came to characterize as a spiritual pilgrimage for those six months. I met with mindfulness teachers but also found myself gravitating toward teachers who spoke of faith and a connectedness to a greater whole.

What I found truly inspired me. I encountered people engaged in contemplation—some including the observation of one's mind and some with a different focus, drawn from ancient practices that predate contemporary mindfulness. Though the latter are not to be conflated or called the same, these ancient rituals and traditions are all practiced within communities—both present communities and those that have existed throughout history. These practices are filled with poetic beauty and embedded within sustained ethics valuing justice for all people and life.

While hiking miles through the chilly mist around a Scottish island on uneven, slick terrain with a Celtic Christian teacher, I learned that a commitment to community and to resistance to empire or oppressive systems generating injustice are inseparable from personal awareness. Sitting at the feet of a Sufi Sheikha in Turkey, I learned that kindness and personal practice are important, but that pure joy is found in devotional practice—understanding oneself not as a separate individual at all, but one with the Divine and all that is greater than oneself. From Buddhist teachers steeped in long lineages, I learned that coming to know one's own mind takes disciplined, ethical practice. From Sikh activists, I learned that present awareness and deep compassionate activism arise from ritual practices coupled with service to persons of any ethnicity—even one's cultural enemies. Resting with an enlightened spiritual friend just arrived from Corfu to live out the last days of her life, I learned that presence comes to us when we let go of fear as well as consumerism and begin to experience space and time in a way that seems to resemble what medieval mystics described simply as being "One."

In these ancient wisdom meditation and prayer practices, self-awakening is never reduced to self-help techniques or severed from ethical consciousness of the world. Nor is it disengaged from a deep sense of spirituality and devotion to a greater Divine or consciousness. Yet, these meditative practices are not readily accessible to the average practitioner. What if, I began to wonder, we partnered the skills gained in mindfulness awareness to lessen our anxiety with the ethical frameworks of ancient traditions? Is there anything to stop us from doing this?

Mindfulness Stumbling Blocks

In fact, I found there was plenty to stop us. The current mindfulness movement is deeply entrenched in our consumerist culture. It can be difficult to discern where mindful awareness opens our eyes and where it is being used by systems to close them and prevent us from seeing the deep, systematic biases of our culture. It is a movement grasping for results—profit, for one, but also results such as reaching increased numbers of individuals with mindfulness; denying aging; self-gratification; and assuming a particular type of "calm" personality.

I discovered that the most frequent claim for mindfulness, coming from serious meditation teachers and frivolous marketing alike, is that it will bring happiness. Interestingly, that happiness is rarely defined. Instead, how you achieve it is carefully outlined. For marketing, that's easy—purchase their product or use their self-help guide. For more serious mindfulness teachers, it centers in methods for inner observation to develop self-awareness and gain equanimity, or more positive reactivity in your life—so that you can be happy regardless of the political, economic, or social conditions of your life or the world around you.

Similarly, there are historically entrenched issues within religious and spiritual traditions preventing a deep dive into that inner awareness and ethical consciousness. In this book I focus mainly on Christianity, which is, for one thing, so mired in the business of keeping its institutions afloat in this political, consumeristic, and secular culture that deep awareness and opening one's eyes to communion with the Divine and developing common humanity often gets lost. There are additional issues we must contend with: some Christian theologies persist that seem to view meditation as almost heretical, carrying one away from knowledge of the Divine. From such perspectives, wisdom is understood to come from an outside authority, and the inner self is not to be trusted. Additionally, we stumble over deeply embedded historic theologies of self-surrender and sacrifice advocated by those in authority, to be adopted by the oppressed. A primary message of Jesus instructing us to side with the oppressed is sometimes suppressed in favor of individualistic theology that awards power over the oppressed to preachers, politicians, and promoters who claim authority in the name of Christ.

Mindfulness and Spiritual Traditions

I believe we need each other—mindfulness practitioners need the ethical underpinnings and devotional stance developed through years within contemplative practices in spiritual traditions. And people of faith need tools like mindful awareness to delve further into that faith and unlock compassionate action in the world.

In this book I invite you to join me in a critical examination of deep biases within the current mindfulness movement, using a framework of critical feminist theory that considers gender, race, and class to delve into this analysis. Additionally, I invite you to imagine what it would mean to feel spiritually grounded and unafraid. And to imagine what depth of compassion we could reach as individuals and as a society, learning to love our neighbors, as ourselves. With clear intention set within a system of ethics valuing all of life, we can even uncover powerful tools for dismantling systems of injustice and bring about awareness for both oppressor and oppressed.

Jim Burklo, author of *Mindful Christianity*,[3] suggests that for those with an orientation or affinity for religious or spiritual practice, secular mindfulness can be an effective "gateway drug" that leads one to dive deeper into religious and spiritual practices.[4] As senior associate dean of religious life at the University of Southern California, he was one of the founders of Mindful USC, which now teaches secular mindfulness to well over seven thousand people a year on the University of Southern California campus.

Burklo acknowledges that mindfulness truly fills a need in our stressed-out society, helping individuals to cope. But, he asserts, it's when he takes groups of students on retreat to a Christian monastery to learn of the great tradition of spiritual devotion that they find their clearer purpose and connection in the world. There, they engage in *lectio/visio divina* (a method of praying with scripture and visual media), which takes them into the "heart of the Christian experience." Sadly, the students have not heard of this rich tradition before. Even the simple act of showing them a huge row of books on Western spirituality astonishes them, Burklo says. "They stand in front of this

---

3. Jim Burklo, *Mindful Christianity* (Haworth, NJ: St. Johann Press, 2017).

4. Jim Burklo, interview by author, Long Beach, CA, August 22, 2019.

bookshelf and go, 'Whoa. Whoa dude. Nobody told us about this.' The Catholic kids, they never heard about any of it. The Protestant kids never heard. The kids that had no religion."[5]

Chapter Outline

This book is a call for us to be mindful about our use and practice of mindfulness—to open our vision to new uses of mindfulness coupled with ethical, spiritual practice. It is a call for intentionality. It is a plea for greater awareness of the actual effect mindfulness is having on our society, and a suggestion that there are ancient traditions that can guide us in that awareness. Part One focuses on mindfulness in the context of American culture. In chapter 1, I describe my own journey into mindfulness and begin to examine its unquestioned ability to bring happiness to individuals, society, and the world, as is often claimed. I weave together what I have learned from my own journey into contemplation and my experience of what benefit simple mindfulness tools can have for individuals. We then begin a critical analysis of mindfulness to ask: In what ways is mindfulness helping break down, or shore up, structures upholding unjust systems of oppression?

In chapter 2, I analyze the social construction of mindfulness from a critical theory lens. I invite you to question with me: How is mindfulness being used, who is using it, and how do its promoters define it? I borrow from critical feminist theory to explore how a concept like mindfulness circulates among the population, and ask the question: When mindfulness is secularized and joined with values of consumerism and individualism, can it truly bring about happiness for the overall good of society?

Chapter 3 looks at the most frequent claim of mindfulness: that it will bring about happiness. Drawing again on critical theory, I question the very idea of happiness as celebrated in our culture. Rather than defining happiness, we explore how its pursuit affects society.

---

5. Jim Burklo, interview by author.

In response to Western society's obsession with seeking happiness, are we upholding consumerist and privileged values of the dominant society by pursuing happiness through mindfulness? We ask, what is the use or function of happiness in our culture?

Chapter 4 turns to the claim that mindfulness will bring about happiness by reducing stress in our lives. But could it be that stress, just like happiness, has culturally constructed meanings for us? We ask, what's the use of stress? Chapter 5 focuses on the use of mindfulness to reveal awareness of emotion. Could it be, also, that the construction of emotion in our culture has uses for social control and promoting normativity? In this analysis, we investigate whether focusing on emotion in mindfulness practice without attention to its cultural construction functions to uphold patriarchal control and white privilege.

In Part Two, I invite you into a journey to discover ways in which mindfulness can be used as a liberating force in culture and society. These approaches do not see the individual as isolated, nor do they pretend that structural injustice will get better just by individuals gaining compassion through mindfulness as self-help. We look at how mindfulness tools are currently being applied, and we imagine ways they can be further incorporated into ethical frameworks missing from most uses of mindfulness today. The advent of COVID-19 and the eruption of the Black Lives Matter movement onto the streets of America shed enormous light on the unequal distribution of happiness, stress, and emotions, including fear from lack of safety in our society.

Chapter 6 highlights just a few of the recent ways mindfulness is being woven into ancient and cultural traditions by Black Americans and by any who are marginalized from the dominant white, male, cisgender norm, to promote individual and communal healing from violence upon ancestors, individuals, and society today.

Mindfulness is popularly associated with Buddhism, both in serious teaching and in marketing today. In chapter 7, I look at whether what is being presented is faithful to Buddhism. What can we learn about mindfulness as it emerges from Buddhist practice? And we consider: Is mindfulness Buddhist, or is Buddhism mindfulness?

Next, I turn to spiritual traditions that draw on ancient practice for inner awareness and that offer deep foundations for social justice. I suggest that these histories are present but not easily accessible today. What happens when we couple them with simple mindfulness tools? Chapter 8 introduces several traditions that include practices that are closely aligned with mindfulness practice: Sufism, Sikhism, and Judaism. I offer my personal encounters with wise teachers in each, to raise the question of how these traditions might offer ethical contexts for mindfulness practice.

We then move more in depth to the religion I am most familiar with, that of my ancestors and of my own life. Chapter 9 explores Centering Prayer in Christianity, suggesting what this practice could gain from—and what it adds to—mindfulness practice. Finally, chapter 10 focuses on justice and civil rights movements within Christianity and ways in which Christian contemplation centers on an ethic of justice. I analyze how Christian contemplative practice can be paired with mindfulness practice, offering an ethical context, so that mindfulness tools can help us awaken to social justice needs.

As I write I have you in mind, and this book is for you if you are a student of mindfulness or interested in mindfulness and take mindfulness seriously. This book is also for you if you are a mindfulness teacher. In this analysis I offer the work of contemporary mindfulness teachers as examples of how mindfulness is being used throughout the culture. I have learned from many of you, and I believe the vast majority have heart-felt and well-meaning intentions toward those they teach. I am convinced, however, that many teachers and serious practitioners have failed to notice the extent to which Western consumerist values have so rapidly and seamlessly become intertwined with the mindfulness movement. We are unaware of the extent to which our mindfulness promotion is perpetuating not only needless consumption but also racial, gendered, and classist oppression that is deeply embedded within Western culture. I believe it is our responsibility to awaken to our complicity and to be much more intentional in our promotion, teaching, and practice of mindfulness. With deep concern about what we are doing with mindfulness, I share this analysis with you.

This book is also for you if you identify as Christian, and for any religious and spiritual persons who are worried about whether today's mindfulness is compatible with your theology and practice. By the time you finish reading, I hope you will find ways in which you might benefit from the tools of mindfulness.

A Spiritual Pilgrimage

When I took a sabbatical to study the mindfulness movement through a critical lens, that journey turned into a spiritual pilgrimage. I entered the world of contemplative spiritual traditions developed over centuries. This book is its own pilgrimage, and I invite you to join me to discover where it takes us. We might be accompanied by a koan from the twelfth-century Zen work *Book of Serenity*:

- Dizang asked Fayan, "Where are you going?"
- Fayan said, "Around on pilgrimage."
- Dizang said, "What is the purpose of pilgrimage?"
- Fayan said, "I don't know."
- Dizang said, "Not knowing is most near."[6]

We embark on this near, intimate pilgrimage, journeying first through serious critical analysis, then into ancient traditions eliciting awe and devotion. We travel in search of knowing, and perhaps ultimately toward not knowing and letting go, through the landscapes of mindfulness and spiritual practice, toward a discovery of wonder.

---

6. "Dizang's 'Nearness,'" in *Book of Serenity* (trans. Thomas Cleary; Boston: Shambhala, 1988), 86.

Part One

Deconstructing Mindfulness

CHAPTER 1

A Journey into Mindfulness

If we truly want to know the secret of soulful travel, we need to believe that there is something sacred waiting to be discovered in virtually every journey.[1]

My senior year of college, Bradley Hanson, a Lutheran pastor and professor of religion at Luther College, traveled to Fairfield, Iowa, to learn Transcendental Meditation (TM) and returned to teach it to me and a small group of his students.[2] Later, I studied Centering Prayer, as presented by Father Thomas Keating, who reclaimed and developed this technique of Christian meditation practiced by medieval contemplatives. With the use of Centering Prayer, once I was a professor and chaplain to college students, I deepened my practice of meditation.

By the time I enrolled in my first Mindfulness-Based Stress Reduction (MBSR) course, I was stunned to find, packaged all in one place, practices for personal awareness that I had gradually learned myself throughout a long journey of meditation experiences. Mindfulness,

---

1. Phil Cousineau, *The Art of Pilgrimage: A Seeker's Guide to Making Travel Sacred* (San Francisco, CA: Conari Press, 2012), 25, Kindle.

2. Mahararishi International University, led by Indian guru Maharishi Mahesh Yogi, had recently relocated from California to Fairfield, Iowa. Professor Hanson's journey into TM and into the practice of Christian meditation is chronicled in Bradley Hanson, *The Call of Silence: Discovering Christian Meditation* (Minneapolis: Augsburg, 1980).

as presented in the eight-week MBSR course, captured some of the profound insights I had discovered sustained meditation could do, including helping me to take a step back and lessen my stress level. Not only could I experience life presently, but I could live with less stress derived from painful memories or from worry about the future. The course was taught by Dave Potter, who I am happy to report still teaches more than a decade later and has placed his MBSR course online, free to anyone who wishes to take it.[3] A certified MBSR instructor, he made it available even before the COVID-19 pandemic (when other courses began to appear online for free).

Classical mindfulness, the type I first learned in that MBSR course, is, of course, better experienced than explained. It is normally introduced as a process of turning your attention to a present focus—your breath, or sensations in the body, or sounds that are occurring right now. This elicits a relaxation response that enables you to be more attentive and mindful and may reduce feelings of stress. It helps you to connect to the moment, rather than getting caught in the distractions of a busy mind, by returning your attention to here and now. If you like, try these simple steps. Take just five minutes if you are not used to meditation.

Mindfulness Breath Exercise

1. Find a comfortable posture. Close your eyes if it is comfortable for you or rest your gaze softly in front of you.
2. Do a brief body scan from head to toe, almost as if you're observing your body by reflecting from the inside out, noticing any sensation or tension. Your jaw may be tight or your shoulders hunched, for example. It can sometimes be helpful to inhale, inviting relaxation, and then to exhale to release tension.
3. Bring your awareness to your breath. Just breathe naturally. Be curious. Notice anything that arises, such as coolness or warmth

---

3. Dave Potter, "Palouse Mindfulness," https://palousemindfulness.com.

in your nostrils, or the expansion or contraction of your chest with each breath.

4. When you notice your attention has wandered (which it will!), gently bring your attention back to your breath. You may be distracted by a thought and even caught in a mental story for a bit, or by a sound. Each time you notice your attention has wandered, try not to judge yourself—it's great that you noticed! You are being mindful. Simply return to your breath and to the present.

A central premise of mindfulness is that we are often not living in the present, which contributes to dissatisfaction and dysfunction. Two Harvard psychologists tested this by creating an app through which they could randomly check in with 2,250 diverse subjects. What they discovered is that almost 50 percent of the time, people are not fully engaged in or paying attention to their present task. Further, they found that even when people were doing an unpleasant task, they claimed to feel happier if they were presently engaged than if they were doing a pleasant one with their mind wandering. [4]

There are many ways to practice being mindfully present. One mindfulness tool is to use any of your senses to anchor yourself in the present. Try any of these:

Anchoring Mindfulness Exercises

- Stop and close your eyes, and just listen. Without getting caught in stories about each sound, let the sounds come and go, just as your thoughts, emotions, and physical sensations come and go.
- Sit or walk and intentionally look around you, really noticing what you see. Notice colors, light, shapes, etc.

---

4. Matthew A. Killingsworth and Daniel T. Gilbert, "A Wandering Mind Is an Unhappy Mind," *Science* 330 no. 6006 (Nov. 12, 2010): 932, https://science.sciencemag.org.

- Eat a snack or meal or drink a cup of tea or coffee, savoring every bite or sip, paying full attention to flavor and sensation. When was the last time you actually tasted your food, without talking to someone, watching TV, or scanning your personal device?
- If you are able, bring attention to the feel of your feet as they touch the ground while you stand, walk, or jog.

Mindfulness can help us to be momentarily more satisfied if we are presently focused. But it also helps us notice just what is happening when our minds are wandering so that we can begin to investigate how it is that we keep reverting to a state of dissatisfaction.

Our minds are often busy creating stories to fill in gaps we might not know, trying to make sense about why something happened in the past or what is going to happen in the future. Let's say a woman I know passes by me and looks toward me with a sour look on her face. I might begin to build a story. "Why did she give me that sour look? She must be mad at me; ah, yes, she must have been talking to our mutual friend, whom I offended during a meeting last week; oh my gosh, they're meeting with my boss in the morning, and they'll tell him how offensive I was," and so on.

If I continue along this line of thinking long enough, because I rent a home from my place of employment in addition to working there, by the end of the day (or more like the middle of the night) in my mind, I am both homeless and jobless. All the while, the friend who looked at me with a sour look may have simply been preoccupied with a headache this morning. Yet, my emotions are boiling. I may be experiencing anxiety, anger, and fear. On top of that, I am having physical symptoms (I can't sleep, and my stomach hurts). All because I believed my own story. Our stories can take us to extremes—I once asked university students in a classroom what arises within them when they send a text message to a new friend asking to meet up with them but get no reply. One woman blurted out, "Self-hatred!"

Another thing that may cause your mind to spin and wander is when a particular person or situation triggers a habitual defensive reaction in your brain. Cognitive psychology teaches us that the human brain is capable of neuroplasticity, or the ability to learn and shift the way it functions. It turns out that you can alter your reactions to a recurring thought or situation.[5] I think of the brain as a forest in which your thoughts often automatically start to run down the widest path. It is well worn because every time you have reacted to a particular trigger in the past, you have taken this same route.

We can experiment by becoming mindful when the triggering thought—or the emotion or bodily sensation that typically accompanies it—first appears. At that moment, we can pause, even if it's just long enough to say to ourselves, "Maybe not this time." By doing this, we take a tentative step toward bushwhacking our way through the forest, creating a new pathway and reacting in a different, healthier way. In time, we blaze a new trail. A new habit develops as our usually negative response gives way to a more positive reaction. But it takes time to create a different, well-worn path, and it takes practice to acknowledge that we have been going down a path that may not be healthy for us. It takes time to accept the negative things in ourselves we aren't so proud of, as well as the positive.

As we move more into mindfulness practice, we observe our *mind state*, meaning thoughts and emotions, in the same way we understand the anchors of bodily sensation or sound or breath. They, too, come and go. And the body, mind, and heart, or emotions, are deeply connected. We become mindful of this connection.

If you will, try this exercise for an illustration of how mindfulness can work. It begins with a mindful entryway and includes moments of mindful awareness.

---

5. Susan L. Smalley and Diana Winston, *Fully Present: The Science, Art, and Practice of Mindfulness* (Philadelphia: Da Capo Press, 2010), 7. See also Rick Hanson, *Hardwiring Happiness: The New Brain Science of Contentment, Calm, and Confidence* (New York: Harmony, 2013); and other works by Rick Hanson.

Head, Heart, Body Exercise

Allow yourself to sit upright but relaxed. Close your eyes if it's comfortable. Bring your attention to your breath and allow yourself to settle. Scan your body from head to toe, noticing anything present, such as comfort, pain, tension, warmth, coolness, etc. Return your attention to your breath.

Invite into your mind a thought of someone or something that is mildly difficult or irritating to you. Take time to allow it to enter your thinking.

Next, drop your attention from your head to your heart (from your thoughts to your emotions). Do you notice any emotion that has arisen since you invited this thought? If so, take a moment to put a label on it. Is it anger, fear, anxiety, or something else?

Drop your attention into your body. Do a short body scan like you did at the beginning of this exercise. Has anything shifted since that first body scan? Is the emotion you just discovered (if you discovered an emotion) showing up anywhere in your body? Did the thought you had cause any physical shift?

Let go and return your attention to your breath.

Once more, I invite you to bring a thought to mind, but this time, let it be something that gives you great joy. Allow it to settle into your thoughts.

Drop your attention from head to heart. You might label the precise emotion you are feeling; is it joy, or love, or excitement?

Scan your body again. Has anything shifted as you have thought about what brings you joy? If you don't notice anything, it's perfectly fine. Let that observation be what you are mindful of. Return to your breath and rest there a moment, then open your eyes.

What did you notice? Did you find there was a connection between your thoughts, emotions, and/or physical sensations? Were there any subtle physical shifts that occurred? You might reflect on the thought that was irritating to you. Ask yourself if the narrative behind the thought—particularly if it involves another person and their motives—is really true. Sometimes when we notice a recurring thought, we see that we are actually taking a small bit of information and blowing it up into a negative story line. We are not resting in the present with what we know.

Who Benefits from Mindfulness?

After I began to practice mindfulness and realized that it was a technique others could benefit from, I entered a year-long Training in Mindfulness Facilitation through the Mindful Awareness Research Center at UCLA. Afterward, I began to teach introductory mindfulness courses on my own university campus, first to faculty and staff, and then to students. I was convinced mindfulness could be taught to persons who were spiritual, religious, or secular, and that it could be taught with integrity. I had learned from teachers of Centering Prayer that troubling thoughts and emotions can arise in meditation, and I believed that teaching mindfulness was something that required experience both in meditation and in counseling. I was confident that my university would do this right, with trained teachers and responsible mindfulness methods.

As I practiced and taught these simple techniques initially, faculty and staff were the most interested in them, and some began meditation practices that became a life habit. Many have told me stories of how mindfulness practice helped them awaken to self-understanding and cope with stress at work or home.

Within a few years, however, undergraduate students made up the bulk of my classes. Many were entering the university with some experience in meditation or mindfulness gained in high school. They drifted in and out throughout the series of classes, with a small number practicing daily.

Yet, some students began to display strange symptoms. As they sat doing basic mindfulness breath and body awareness and observing their thoughts and emotions, their anxiety was rising, not falling—to the point of inability to function. Mindfulness practice was not helping to lower their stress. Knowing that past traumas can emerge when a person becomes still in mindfulness practice, I asked them to take a break. I offered resources for these students to seek counseling and to try movement practices. Physical exercise, like yoga or workouts, helped some but not all these individuals. Since that time, fortunately, practices for dealing with trauma and mindfulness have emerged, and skilled teachers have developed exercises with the potential to bring healing in such cases.[6]

Other students seemed to get caught in a kind of depression and drifted away from mindfulness. Even though mindfulness did help shift their thinking somewhat, nothing in the conditions of their lives shifted. They still lived with racist aggression every day. They still juggled work, classes, and enormous looming student-loan debts. They still suffered with family members who lost their jobs and health insurance. They were still caught in abusive circumstances. Mindfulness teachers might say that as their awareness of their suffering gets better, they will become able to change their circumstances. Yet, these conditions are set within a racist, misogynist, homophobic culture that itself requires a culture shift. We will return to the question of the role and claims of mindfulness amid these conditions in the coming chapters.

Who Teaches Mindfulness?

I soon discovered that there were some staff members on my campus who were teaching with no mindfulness experience of their own. I met a woman who had recently been hired to do wellness programming with university students. She was a bright, very engaging young woman. She shared with me that she wanted to offer mindfulness to all students. I was pleased and asked her about her mindfulness practice. My question was greeted with silence. I learned she had neither training nor experience with the practice of mindfulness. My encounter with her was only one of many. I realized that people with no training were relying on mindfulness apps to teach rooms full of people.

---

6. See, for example, David A. Treleavan, *Trauma-Sensitive Mindfulness: Practices for Safe and Transformative Healing* (New York: W. W. Norton, 2018).

The urgency to teach mindfulness to as many individuals as quickly as possible was fueled by the enthusiasm of the press surrounding results from psychology, communication, and neuroscience research. Indeed, as we have noted, scientific studies were demonstrating that practices like mindfulness could shift our mental capacity toward less reactivity and greater calm. Even more articles claiming to be based on scientific evidence were emerging by the thousands, touting the many benefits of mindfulness. Along with anecdotal stories of lonely lives turned around, workers finding greater satisfaction, and companies showing increased productivity through mindfulness, the media seemed to imply that any means necessary should be used to teach mindfulness to the masses.

Backed up by science, sponsored by profit-minded companies, and spread through social media, mindfulness teachers quickly became celebrities. Endorsements of the power of mindfulness seemed to appear almost out of nowhere in a daily barrage of tweets, blogs, social media posts, book promotions, and expensive retreats. Articles, books, advertisements, and podcasts claimed that elimination of individual stress in favor of inner peace and vibrancy comes through mastering mindfulness practices for mindful eating, mindful parenting, mindful selling, mindful working, and mindful sex, to name just a small fraction of popular current applications.

Decades ago, Jon Kabat-Zinn, whom many regard as the father of the contemporary mindfulness movement, began the Stress Reduction and Relaxation Program at the University of Massachusetts Medical School to harness the tools of mindfulness for acknowledging and attaching less to one's pain, thus living more freely even amid illness. He insisted on a high standard of training for teachers, based on systematic and rigorous mindfulness training.[7] Kabat-Zinn went on to develop the Mindfulness-Based Stress Reduction (MBSR) program, mentioned earlier in this chapter,

---

7. Jon Kabat-Zinn, *Full Catastrophe Living* (New York: Bantam Books, 2013), 2.

which encompasses many of the practices of classical mindfulness training.[8] Diana Winston, director of mindfulness education at the UCLA Mindful Awareness Research Center (MARC), remains concerned that coaching individuals to develop this ability to pay attention to the present moment requires well-trained teachers. The MARC Training in Mindfulness Facilitation program, which has trained hundreds of mindfulness facilitators over the past decade (I was a graduate in one of the early years), involves a year-long commitment to intellectual and practical training.[9] Winston has also recently collaborated on the development of a national certification for mindfulness teachers.[10]

Mindfulness Emerges in the West

One of the most widely circulated definitions of mindfulness is "paying attention to our present-moment experiences with openness, curiosity, and a willingness to be with what is."[11] Classical definitions of contemporary mindfulness suggest that you are engaged in mindfulness when you are intentionally paying attention to whatever is happening to you at any given moment. You do this while at the same time holding an attitude of tenderness or kindness toward, yet withholding judgment of, everything that enters your awareness. This practice can bring awareness of experiences of physical pain and emo-

---

8. A note on terminology—mindfulness teacher Diana Winston uses the term "classical mindfulness meditation" to refer to vipassana practice, but for our purposes I am using the term "classical mindfulness" not to refer to a system of practice, like vipassana practice within Buddhism, but as a set of tools used to bring one more mindfully into the present. See Winston, *The Little Book of Being: Practices and Guidance for Uncovering Your Natural Awareness* (Boulder, CO: SoundsTrue, 2019), 5.

9. Diana Winston, interview by author, UCLA, Los Angeles, CA, August 21, 2019.

10. Mindful Awareness Research Center, https://www.uclahealth.org; International Mindfulness Teachers Association, www.imta.org.

11. Winston, *The Little Book of Being*, 28.

tions such as fear, sadness, or despair, as well as joy, calm, and pleasure.

There are many works introducing readers to the development of what we now know as *mindfulness* in the United States. Wakoh Shannon Hickey, for example, researches the uses of meditation as medicine by tracing a prior, centuries-old tradition developed and led largely by women. Her book *Mind Cure* offers a fascinating history that combines scientific study of mindfulness with Buddhist practice, setting the stage for the development of MBSR by Kabat-Zinn in 1979. This is just one of the rich resources offering history and analysis of this movement.[12]

Mindfulness and Science

While the foundations of mindfulness have been around for some time, it is the marriage of mindfulness with science under a secular banner that has catapulted it into one of the best-known self-help techniques on the market today. When I began teaching mindfulness, I noted that this was the first time in my life I had seen science corroborating religion. Practices pulled from centuries of religious traditions were being studied, with brain scientists concluding that the practices actually shift the way the human brain works.

The results from scientific studies of mindfulness are quite remarkable. As I mentioned earlier in this chapter, scientists now understand that our brains are more malleable than was once thought—that they can be retrained, in part through meditation. Many researchers study what I call the Olympiads of Meditation. These include persons like Matthieu Ricard who have dedicated their lives to a monastic life

---

12. Wakoh Shannon Hickey, *Mind Cure: How Meditation Became Medicine* (New York: Oxford University Press, 2019). See also Philip Goldberg, *American Veda: From Emerson and the Beatles to Yoga and Meditation—How Indian Spirituality Changed the West* (New York: Harmony Books, 2010); Jeff Wilson, *Mindful America: The Mutual Transformation of Buddhist Meditation and American Culture* (New York: Oxford University Press, 2014); and Ann Gleig, *American Dharma: Buddhism Beyond Modernity* (New Haven, CT: Yale University Press, 2019).

of Buddhist meditation; many of them have practiced ten thousand hours or more.

With the exile of His Holiness the Dalai Lama and his community from their native Tibet in 1959, Buddhist meditation practice ceased to belong to a single area and began to disseminate across the world. The Dalai Lama met Western scientists and encouraged them to study "happiness" and "positive emotions" as fervently as they had previously studied such subjects as depression and anxiety.[13] The challenge raised by the Dalai Lama was to bring together ways of studying consciousness as objectively observed through rigorous scientific method studying purely physical states and as subjectively experienced and observed through rigorously regulated Buddhist introspective meditation. He has worked with the scientific community to combine these vastly different methods toward a fuller study of consciousness.[14] He refers to mindfulness as a science itself, and this claim is often repeated by mindfulness teachers today.

What Happened to Mindfulness?

There have been many criticisms raised about just what has happened to mindfulness since it entered the West. For example, Buddhist practitioners criticize the exclusive use of scientific justifications as a motivation for mindfulness practice, especially the emphasis on seeing mindfulness as a tool for continual progress and improvement. When proponents of mindfulness fundamentally focus on what one gains from mindfulness practice, its purpose becomes all about goal achievement for individual practitioners.[15] Its spiritual roots are lost.

---

13. Matthieu Ricard, *Happiness: A Guide to Developing Life's Most Important Skill* (trans. Jesse Browner; New York: Little, Brown, 2006), 186–201.

14. His Holiness the Dalai Lama, *The Universe in a Single Atom: The Convergence of Science and Spirituality* (New York: Morgan Road Books, 2005).

15. Marc R. Poirier, "Mischief in the Marketplace for Mindfulness," in Barry Magid and Robert Rosenbaum, *What's Wrong with Mindfulness*

Ironically, mindfulness largely grew out of a tradition that eschewed the pursuit of any personal goal. Vipassana is a school within the Theravada tradition of Buddhism, one that privileges meditation more than some forms of Buddhism and has been a main source for today's mindfulness meditation technique. Mindfulness practice spawned largely from this school; as you practice, you gain enlightenment into the truth of what *is*. If you practice with another goal in mind, you are missing the point.

Indeed, vipassana teachers I have sat in retreats with, such as Rebecca Bradshaw and Greg Scharf, often repeat in their instructions that if you are seeking a particular experience or state, you are wandering from your true purpose in meditation.[16] In vipassana meditation, a Buddhist practice that is a central root of mindfulness practice, the concept of *equanimity* refers to the ability to be with what is present, whether unpleasant or pleasant, without resistance to it. It is an opportunity to learn to live with life as it is and to live one's life fully in the present.

Criticisms of contemporary mindfulness are leveled by academic researchers as well, also centering on the purposes and uses of mindfulness. The notion of "presence," as cultivated by corporate managers, has been said to be paramount to a new labor concept in the service of capitalist performance and goals.[17] It has become a necessary practice for employees and harnessed for the clear purpose of greater production. This is often disguised as a crucial tool for creating a harmonious working environment; managers encourage a kinder, more cooperative workplace, which they say will be fostered by individual practices

---

(And What Isn't): Zen Perspectives (Somerville, MA: Wisdom Publications, 2016), 13–27.

16. Talks by Rebecca Bradshaw, Greg Scharf, and other vipassana teachers are available at www.dharmaseed.org.

17. Jaana Parviainen and Ilmari Kortelainen, "Becoming Fully Present in Your Body: Analysing Mindfulness as an Affective Investment in Tech Culture," *Somatechnics* 9, nos. 2–3 (2019): 353–75, www.euppublishing.com/soma.

such as mindfulness. The expectation is that happier, more focused workers will mean enhanced productivity and, ultimately, increased profits.

While mindfulness is often claimed to be goalless by meditation teachers and to help people to simply live in the present, in the West it is often marketed as a commodity, embedded with purposes and goals associated with consumer and corporate profit. These purposes and goals are further embedded in a culture of privilege, where some are entitled to that profit and others left out. As we continue with Part One, we explore the current motivations for uses of mindfulness in the United States. Is mindfulness used for specific goals? What are the uses of mindfulness in our culture today?

Chapter 2

What's the Use of Mindfulness?

What one finds in mindful meditation, it turns out, is what one sought before beginning the practice, and the benefits that result . . . are determined by specific cultural and other factors.[1]

To begin to understand mindfulness and its uses in the West, especially the United States, I vowed to simply follow mindfulness around, rather than try to corral and define it. I set out to observe some of the ways mindfulness is being used, beginning with claims of what it will do for those who practice it.

I went to a Mindfulness Exposition at the Anaheim Convention Center near Disneyland, where I attended workshops with titles such as "A Journey of Self-Love"; "An Experience of You"; "Vibe High with Your Future Self"; "Transform Your Life"; "Finding Your Passion"; and "Spiritual Selling." As these titles reveal, the message for consumers is that mindfulness can be applied to exciting and blissful experiences of self-actualization, and that it can even be financially lucrative.

For instance, just as workshop presenters applied to give workshops at the Mindfulness Expo, exhibitors applied for the opportunity to set up displays in its exhibit hall. These vendors were selling beauty products, massage and holistic health experiences, crystal-encrusted

---

1. Jeff Wilson, *Mindful America: The Mutual Transformation of Buddhist Meditation and American Culture* (New York: Oxford University Press, 2014), 121.

jewelry, full-body transformational wellness coaching, CBD products, books on "spiritual selling," spandex wear for Kundalini, self-realization teachings, and bags of rocks mined from a mountain to place under your pillow at night (to block the harmful effects of cell-phone frequencies in your bedroom)!

Salespersons at two booths used similar methods to demonstrate the effectiveness of the product they were selling: applying pressure to my forearm and asking me to resist with all my strength, as they either pointed a laser at my chest or put their hand on my forehead. A third requested to put my forearm into a scanner for fifteen minutes. Each of these was supposed to result immediately in better balance, clearer thinking, and more emotional regulation. Repeated use of his product, one salesperson told me, would heal any psoriasis, age spots, joint pain, or migraines I may experience, help me lose weight if needed, and would drastically increase my overall energy level. Any of these products would eliminate negativity, give me back my time, and, in short, my life.

Not one of the booths—which were also selling organic vegetables, purified, electrified water ("we've succeeded in bottling the energy of lightning," I was told), and even new window frames for your home—included the word *mindfulness* in their product name or exhibit title. Yet, each of these organizations applied for exhibit space at a Mindfulness Expo. Curious, I asked salespeople how their product was related to mindfulness. They replied that mindfulness today really just means "wellness," or that mindfulness is about "self-actualization," or that mindfulness is being "thoughtful" or "mindful" and thus reaching our "full personal potential." This is achievable, they said, through the use of their products for mere tens, hundreds, and, in several cases, thousands of dollars for even a single trial use.

The Mindfulness Expo was organized by Michelle Zarrin, a practitioner of mindfulness meditation, out of her sincere desire for all people to discover their true purpose. A workshop she led was the only one whose description indicated that meditation may not always be pleasant but takes time and careful practice. Michelle shared with me her desire that mindfulness be available to everyone, which was readily apparent as the event was both accessible and affordable.[2]

Mindfulness is also being touted as useful for helping people live healthier lives and lowering their stress level. A recent special edition of *Time* magazine focused on mindfulness and included articles intended to help you to center yourself amid an open-office environment, lower stress in a big-box store line, and love your body parts (including your butt, hips, and thighs). Notably, the articles shy away from challenging the reasons for the stress itself, such as what we are even doing in big-box store lines or worrying over those specific body parts and how we look as we age. One article featured neuroscience research carried out at a Buddhist-based retreat center. It is notable work focused on gauging the effects of meditation on the immune system and heart health. Yet, the article summarizes the potential effects of the research with a profound question we all have uppermost in our minds: "Could this mean a heavy dose of mindfulness might be a better investment than Botox?"[3] Botox is not primarily known for lengthening your life or improving your health. The takeaway, apparently, is that mindfulness can improve your health while offering you the same effects as an injection that reduces wrinkles so you will look younger than you really are.

Mindfulness is marketed to teach *you*, whoever you are, to appear more youthful; love yourself; find your passion; feel vibrant and alive; create the existence you've always wanted; and live in a state of peace and love. Mindfulness has immense healing powers, and if you practice, it will transform your own life, as well as transforming no less than the entire world.

It may feel like I'm just being petty in listing these examples. But

---

2. Michele Zarrin, interview by author, Anaheim, CA, November 30, 2019.

3. Katherine Ellison, "The New Mindfulness: Living. Thinking. Being," *Time* Special Edition (2019): 24–27. The article featured the work of Clifford Saron of the University of California Davis at Spirit Rock Retreat Center.

these claims of transforming you, your life, and the world are made by those selling products as well as by serious mindfulness teachers. Almost universally, claims are being made that taking a course in mindfulness will enable you to transform your life and the world. I submit that such lofty claims can be quite confusing for the average consumer.

The Construction of Mindfulness

Is mindfulness just one more self-help technique that keeps people focused on the self rather than on shared societal problems? Is it becoming an "opiate for the people"? I asked around to see if anyone else noticed or shared my fear. Jack Kornfield, one of the early proponents, innovators, and best-known teachers in today's mindfulness movement, replied to me, "Of course . . . we're Americans, we know how to misuse anything!"[4]

I wholeheartedly agreed with him. But, as I began to see, there is something sinister occurring that goes beyond misuse. The Mindfulness Expo whose exhibit display I described was just the tip of the iceberg. Mindfulness was truly being geared toward the "haves" who already gain from our consumerist society. On a larger scale, Wisdom 2.0 had already emerged as a premier national mindfulness conference. Held annually in San Francisco, it attracts business executives, technology workers, lawyers, yoga enthusiasts, mindfulness teachers, and more.

I attended Wisdom 2.0 several years in a row to gain material for my research on mindfulness. It cost thousands of dollars to attend, by the time I paid the hefty registration fee, purchased airline and airport-to-hotel transportation, stayed at the downtown San Francisco Hilton, and ate at downtown San Francisco restaurants. Add to that the temptation (if you could afford it) to spend hundreds more, if not another thousand, on a spectacular, mindful piece of jewelry,

---

4. Jack Kornfield, interview by author, Santa Monica, CA, July 28, 2019.

among many other items sold at the conference's exhibit-hall booths. Sandwiched between displays promoting mindfulness courses and companies were booths that took a stretch of the imagination to understand what they had to do with practicing mindfulness, just as I had observed at the Mindfulness Expo. This is not to minimize the power of rock or earth from which crystal jewelry is mined or made, but to point out that these and other expensive products were intended to attract higher-class buyers. Here, I could choose a beautiful necklace featuring the crystal of the month that would help manifest every new chapter, dream, and vision in my life; or find an exquisite set of earrings handcrafted in Bali, advertised with the promise that with this purchase, presumably by wearing the jewelry, I was guaranteed to discover my own truth. If you were so inclined and had the resources, it seemed, you could buy yourself a peaceful and authentic life.

Speakers at the 2020 Wisdom 2.0 conference included CEOs, mindfulness teachers, celebrities, politicians, and political organizers tackling subjects like loneliness in a digital age, mindful leadership, and discovering our inner wisdom. In 2020, more political organizers and Black Americans speaking on social impact and healing racism were invited to speak than in previous years. And organizers made a point of informing the majority gathered that some in our midst had received scholarships in order to guarantee access and increase our diversity.

Yet, a deeply troubling dynamic that had been playing out in previous conferences continued to churn beneath the surface. It centers on the lack of "mindful attention" paid to the societal and particularly economic inequities and conditions undergirding the lives of those the conference caters to, or more accurately, does not cater to. Longtime Buddhist meditator and teacher Ronald Purser describes such a moment during the 2014 Wisdom 2.0 Conference. Activists from San Francisco succeeded in disrupting the main stage with a protest against the gentrification and displacement of permanent residents with the emergence of Google and tech giants in the city. As soon as they were removed, a Google executive on the stage calmed the crowd, leading them in a few mindful moments, then returned to the business at hand of developing the mindfulness skills of the tech workers and other participants.

Those who might protest any potential negative effects on our society from companies incorporating mindfulness in their workplaces were "mindfully managed out of meaningful existence." When such troublesome issues come up, the mindful answer is to just keep calm, breathe, and center yourself in the present, acknowledging that there is discomfort in the world; then you can peacefully return to "business as usual."[5]

By Wisdom 2.0 in 2020, however, I noticed a shift in the tone of the presentations: there was more championing of how mindfulness would change society, and even the world, through social change. More examples of small groups, firms, or community organizers applying mindfulness to address particular social problems were highlighted. Yet, from the main stage, organizers felt the need to warn those of us in attendance how to be savvy and avoid difficulty when we exited the conference hotel and encountered homeless persons. I felt as though the organizers were including me and the thousands in attendance in a club whose members would understand that some in society had not yet achieved our place of mindful privilege and that we needed to be careful and even fearful of them. There was still no guidance from the main stage as to how mindfulness might assist in dealing with issues facing the unhoused or the general lack of housing in downtown San Francisco.[6]

---

5. Ronald Purser, *McMindfulness: How Mindfulness Became the New Capitalist Spirituality* (Marquette, MI: Repeater, 2019), 180, Kindle. For additional discussion of this incident at Wisdom 2.0, see Kevin Healey, "Disrupting Wisdom 2.0: The Quest for Mindfulness in Silicon Valley and Beyond," *Journal of Religion, Media and Digital Culture* 4, no. 1 (2015): 67–95.

6. After noticing this trend at Wisdom 2.0 in 2020, I discovered this criticism had been raised as long ago as 2013. See Purser, *McMindfulness*, 181.

In 2021, because of the ongoing pandemic, the entire conference was online. It was the first time I felt that the content was given more importance than the context. While I know the in-person conference is an amazing opportunity for many to connect with one another around mindful investing, teaching, and living, it is also weighed down with materialism and capitalism.

Another more recently organized online conference, the Mindfulness & Compassion Summit, featured online booths for sponsors of the summit that specifically claimed to engage with mindfulness. While a few such sponsors were organizations that genuinely gather communities to meditate in a Buddhist vein and serve their communities, such as InsightLA, most were either for-profit or nonprofit businesses. These were advertised as organizations that will help to inspire, guide, and connect individuals and corporations. They will assist everyone wanting to explore mindfulness, whether to improve relationships, health, or a compassionate society. They will help corporations grow their companies powerfully. The marketing was ingenious. I am still unpacking one statement in which a company claimed that, based on science from multiple scientific fields (all listed in the ad), it would help persons and companies "approach their full potential by creating consistent and visible outer impact through proactive inner mastery."[7]

Large corporations, many of which were represented at Wisdom 2.0 and the Mindfulness & Compassion Summit, now regularly invest in mindfulness programs. Some have created programs for their employees and market their successes by offering programs for other companies, such as Google's Search Inside Yourself. Others are encouraged by the likes of *Forbes* magazine to hire "neurocoaches" to assist employees to "discover the layers within their brain."[8] Reasons given for introducing mindfulness in the workplace include focus-

---

7. From advertisement for InnerMBA—see www.innermba.com.

8. Stephanie Burns, "Can Mindfulness Help You Run Your Business?" *Forbes*, August 29, 2019, https://www.forbes.com.

ing on problems of decreasing worker stress and exhaustion, increasing worker satisfaction, limiting worker turnover, and expanding researcher creativity. For many, the bottom line is that mindfulness programs add up to a positive return on investment and a competitive advantage in the marketplace.[9]

If you believe the advertisements we've described so far, uses of mindfulness include healing all your physical ailments, mastering your inner self, manifesting a successful future self, and increasing your production and earnings. But this is not all it's said to be good for.

Mindfulness and Compassion

A serious and central claim of mindfulness is that it will help you to develop compassion. Add to that the claim that as you practice mindfulness, you will be participating in the transformation of society as a whole. Advertising for one online mindfulness course claims: "You'll learn valuable mindfulness skills and tools . . . all while you experience the power of awareness to transform your life *and the world*."[10] Mindfulness teachers rely on neuroscience studies demonstrating that practicing mindfulness can help stimulate compassion centers of the brain. Their instructions often begin with exercises to develop compassion for yourself, encouraging self-care. From there, it is claimed, you will begin to extend that compassion to people around you, first within your own community and then to wider and wider circles of care.

One thing I find fascinating is the increasingly deliberate appearance of the word *compassion* along with *mindfulness*, such as the Mindfulness & Compassion Summit I referred to earlier. The practice of mindfulness alone clearly has not automatically equated to

---

9. "5 Reasons Your Company Should Be Investing in Mindfulness Training," *Inc.*, October 17, 2019, https://www.inc.com.

10. Sounds True, "The Power of Awareness," https://product.sounds true.com/power-of-awareness, emphasis mine.

compassion in people's minds, as the word compassion needs to be explicitly stated up front. Individuals may find, as neuroscience shows, that they develop more empathy as they increase attention in their own lives. Yet it is clear, and this may be in spite of early mindfulness teachers' assumptions, that the way our society has absorbed mindfulness has not led to an increase in compassionate service or to any deep understanding of the need to rectify the unequal distribution of suffering in society.

Thankfully, some teachers and leaders of mindfulness are tackling these issues, particularly in light of the Black Lives Matter movement. Leading up to the massive protests in the summer of 2020, they had already begun taking seriously challenges of unconscious bias in the mindfulness movement. Rhonda Magee, mindfulness teacher and professor of law, was a featured leader at Mindfulness & Trauma, a conference I attended in 2019 at the Omega Institute in New York. She has pioneered work on mindfulness, diversity, and inclusion, and she led the conference participants in mindful exercises to uncover implicit racial bias. She has developed specific exercises aimed at compassion for one another, as well as for understanding social biases that block compassion.[11]

Mindfulness organizations dedicated to racial justice have been operating in pockets across the country for some years and have been able to couple compassion with justice in mindfulness, particularly through the incorporation of Buddhist teachings. One of the longest-standing Buddhist organizations to offer mindfulness to people who are Black, Indigenous, and People of Color (BIPOC) is East Bay Meditation Center (EMBC) in Oakland, California. EBMC has trained many People of Color as meditation teachers. Other organizations have been increasingly offering mindfulness retreat opportunities specifically for LBGTQIA+ and BIPOC retreatants, including Spirit Rock Meditation Center in Woodacre, California.

---

11. "Mindfulness & Trauma," Omega Institute, Rhinebeck, NY, August 2–4, 2019.

EBMC continues a practice, as do some individual teachers at Spirit Rock and other vipassana meditation centers across the country, of ensuring that mindfulness is accessible to a wide array of practitioners. This is accomplished by having teachers accept only donations for their work, rather than charging a set fee. Wishing to remain true to the dharma, the teachings of the Buddha, these teachers pledge to operate only by receiving *dana,* or donations. This stems from a centuries-old understanding derived from Asian cultures that one never sells the teachings of the Buddha. This ethic is admirable and difficult in Western culture, and clearly does not make these teachers or organizations financial success stories.

This is beyond ironic, as these same teachings have brought enormous financial success for others. It is in large part the teaching of the dharma by these very teachers that has led to the spread of mindfulness, which has in turn produced enormously popular mindfulness apps in the past decade. It is estimated, for example, that the apps Calm, Headspace, and Ten Percent Happier all bring in millions of dollars in revenue, with Calm netting over a billion dollars.[12]

Considering this, we return to the question of a possible link between mindfulness and compassion. Is the enormous success of mindfulness in the marketplace creating a more compassionate society? The idea that mindfulness, as it is used today, will transform society has been referred to as "magical thinking."[13] Zen teacher Robert Meikyo Rosenbaum notes,

> The point here is that becoming more mindful only in the restricted sense of being "more attentive" of your surroundings and of your thoughts, emotions, and perceptions does not tap into the depths of meditation practice. Being "more attentive" while clinging to a sense of yourself as a separate, independent

---

12. "Calm, the 7–Year-Old Meditation App Says It's Now Valued at $1 Billion," *Insider*, February 6, 2019, https://www.businessinsider.com.

13. Ronald Purser, interview with author, San Diego, CA, November 25, 2019.

being will not necessarily make you a better person any more than solving a koan will prevent you from becoming depressed or completing a thousand prostrations will make it easier for you to drive to work in the morning.[14]

In other words, practicing mindfulness in your corporate setting or other consumption-minded context will no more create a compassionate society than taking a deep breath will cement your commitment to improving air quality and fighting climate change.

Is Mindfulness Working?

As I say to groups when I am asked to offer an introduction to mindfulness, there are many definitions and multiple uses of mindfulness. Some people, as we have seen, believe mindfulness simply means you are being thoughtful and mindful in daily activities. Others use it as a marketing technique meant to entice you to purchase anything from snacks to dermatology insurance. Then there is mindfulness meditation, which, when practiced, may actually help to shift brain patterns. We will touch on many more uses of mindfulness in the chapters to come. But one question we might ask is: Are people at least more mindful in their daily lives?

We need not sit and wonder, because as many uses as there are for mindfulness, there are also plenty of instruments on the market to measure their outcomes. Mindfulness is particularly marketed, sold, and measured by how individuals engaging in it progress toward being more mindful and present in their daily lives. Particular populations targeted by such marketing include corporate employees and college students.

More and more scientific research is emerging that measures, using neurological measurements, the effects of mindfulness and other

---

14. Robert Meikyo Rosenbaum, "'I' Doesn't Mind," in Robert Meikyo Rosenbaum and Barry Magid, eds., *What's Wrong with Mindfulness and What Isn't: Zen Perspectives* (Somerville, MA: Wisdom Publications), 36.

meditation and prayer practices on the physical brain. This type of research holds great promise for our future understanding of the effectiveness of mindfulness as a tool for neuroenhancement, or training the brain.[15] Yet there are far more subjective instruments popularly in use to measure the effects of mindfulness. One of the more widespread is the Mindful Attention Awareness Scale (MAAS), which assesses the differences in enhanced mindful attention, or attention to present experience, over time. Initially, the instrument was designed to measure whether long-term mindfulness practices result in greater present focus. Initial subjects tested were highly experienced meditators, such as life-long Zen practitioners.

Researchers Kirk Brown and Richard Bryan concluded that measuring mindfulness is solely about determining one's awareness of one's present state. They discovered from the Zen meditators that whether one is currently meditating did not seem to be as much of a factor in their higher mindfulness scores as how many years one had practiced. Results showed that long-term practice (i.e., years of experience, and tens of thousands of hours of meditation) was what made the difference as to whether the subjects were truly more mindful and focused on the present. Mindfulness is purposeless in the sense that it is not about achieving immediate well-being, according to Brown and Ryan.[16] Their conclusions support earlier studies, showing that having a particular purpose or goal in mind (to feel good, to be patient, to move past anger, etc.) would only limit an individual's awareness of their present state.

However, instruments like the MAAS survey are also used today in ways that are precisely geared toward measuring how much progress one has made toward paying attention after engaging in just a

---

15. See Amir Raz and Sheida Rabipour, *How (Not) to Train the Brain: Enhancing What's between Your Ears With (and Without) Science* (New York: Oxford University Press, 2019), and other works by Raz.

16. K. W. Brown and R. M. Ryan, "The Benefits of Being Present: Mindfulness and Its Role in Psychological Well-being," *Journal of Personality and Social Psychology* 84, no. 4 (April 2003): 822–48, https://psycnet.apa.org.

short, current meditation practice.[17] We might call these *purposive* outcomes, or the kind of outcomes that the contemporary mindfulness market claims will be the result of your mindfulness practice.

The MAAS survey asks fifteen questions about how present or distracted you are in your life while engaging in certain tasks, such as driving or eating, and how aware you are of your current emotions and physical state. The last time I used this instrument with students in a semester-long course in mindfulness (before I read the original MAAS research study), the average score as reported by the students at the end of the semester almost exactly matched that of experienced Zen meditators in the original MAAS study. I do not consider myself an expert meditator, but I am more experienced than my students. Thus, I was surprised when I scored significantly lower than they did on the survey.

There may be good reasons for why the university students scored themselves higher. For instance, more experienced meditators note that they are aware of how quickly the state of mind jumps from moment to moment, and just how distracted their minds can be.[18] Additionally, the students may be reacting to the messages they hear and see about mindfulness all around them, which continually highlight its multiple short-term benefits.

When mindfulness is used for such divergent purposes as we have noted, including increasing our personal and corporate competitive edge, all the brain science in the world showing its effect on one brain at a time cannot assure us that the mindfulness currently being marketed in our culture is going to bring about an equitable, compassionate society. With notable exceptions, mindfulness serves brilliantly as a self-help technique for individuals seeking ways to cope within our stressed-out, production-oriented, and profit-driven society—hence, its popularity. But it does little to challenge the societal values

---

17. Brown and Ryan, "The Benefits of Being Present," 844.

18. Wakoh Shannon Hickey, *Mind Cure: How Meditation Became Medicine* (New York: Oxford University Press, 2019), 178.

that give rise to the need for it and that enable its massive marketing efforts.

It's easy to claim that mindfulness is working to help people bring about particular effects in their lives. And the dominant claim of mindfulness marketing is that it will bring you happiness. So as we develop an understanding of the conscious agenda behind marketing today, we turn to this question: Does mindfulness really bring happiness to everyone (or anyone)?

CHAPTER 3

Mindfulness Will Bring
You Happiness

The face of happiness . . . looks rather like the face of privilege. . . .
To track the history of happiness is to track the history of its distri-
bution.[1]

For years, I gave an example from my own life about how a simple
mindfulness exercise can help you be more at ease and happier as
you move about in various cultural contexts. Several times a year, I
am invited through my work to attend events sponsored by a philanthropic women's organization that is populated by women in the
top echelon of society. In the early years, I would enter beautifully
appointed dining rooms in luxury hotels for a champagne brunch
or an afternoon tea filled with women of means and fashion. No
matter how careful I was in selecting what I wore, I felt terribly self-
conscious. So, I explained to mindfulness students, I began to use this
as an experiment in mindfulness.

As I entered, I would slide to the side of the room, scan the bustling
energy in the room as women in stunning designer clothing greeted
one another. I would take just a few moments to do a Three Center

---

1. Sara Ahmed, *The Promise of Happiness* (Durham, NC: Duke University Press, 2010), 11, 19.

Check-In mindfulness exercise,[2] scanning what was happening in my
head, my heart, and my body. I asked myself: What thoughts are in
my head? (I noticed thoughts like "I am frumpy" and "I am inadequate.") Second, what is in my heart, or what emotions are present?
(In this situation, I felt discomfort and unease.) Finally, I reflected on
what was going on in my body (I sensed that my stomach was tight,
and my shoulders were hunched.)

After three or four years of doing this check-in at least twice a
year, I excitedly reported to mindfulness students, I was rid of my
self-consciousness—to the point that I eventually walked into one of
these events, did a mindful Three Center Check-In scan, and no self-
consciousness arose. Success!

Mindfulness meditation instructions say to notice emotion, and
whether it is pleasant or unpleasant, without judgment. If you feel
discomfort, work with it. Recognize the thought that accompanies
it and accept the actual feeling of discomfort. Next, investigate it a
bit—are you feeling self-consciousness, or guilt, or pain, for example? Then, notice where you might feel it in your body. The goal is to
notice the discomfort and stay with it, then release attachment to the
feeling and move on. You may discover, after developing a heightened
self-awareness combined with the ability to step back and let go, that
the discomfort will lessen.

I love that I can learn, with mindful tools, to be comfortable in
situations I sometimes need to step into. I love that those three short
steps allow me to step outside myself enough to come to know some
of the women in this organization, to value them as friends, and to
appreciate beauty, pain, and humanity within them. This is in no way
a negative comment on any individuals I met at these events; I am
honored to know them.

However, I now realize there was nothing inappropriate at all in
my feeling uncomfortable at those events, and that the discomfort

---

2. I first learned this meditation exercise from Buddhist meditation
teacher Pamela Weiss.

was not something solely created in my own mind. I love getting dressed up. I always have, ever since I was a child, such as when I got to go to church in a new Sunday dress in my favorite color, red, that my mother had just sewn for me. But coveting what others have and feeling inadequate, feeling if I only had what they have to wear it would add to my own happiness, is another thing altogether.

Yet, everything around me teaches me to be uncomfortable so that I will desire expensive clothing and jewelry and designer labels. Having those things will bring me happiness. This message fills our culture and the air I breathe. Our American economic system thrives on you and me seeking fashion-current wardrobes and striving along this never-ending, upwardly mobile trajectory of consumption. You and I know that wealth and fashion do not equal happiness, yet they are such societally ingrained symbols of what will bring happiness, we almost can't help but chase after them. We do this even though we know that (1) wealth and fashion amount to an inappropriate paradigm for happiness for the vast majority of people; (2) far less than 1 percent of the population will achieve wealth vast enough to be able to afford everything we dream of buying; and (3) getting a bargain on clothing often means we are buying from companies with questionable labor practices, and no one truly needs new clothing for every occasion.

Interestingly, the last time I offered this example, a young woman in class commented on the fact that I am invited to those philanthropic events because of my professional position in my organization. "Maybe the women there are feeling intimidated by you," she offered. I had not thought of that. And if she is right, what would be the cause of their discomfort? Could it be that not all women, even the wealthiest, have had the opportunity to pursue their intellectual passions as I have, in our patriarchal culture? Might their discomfort also be appropriate?

What's the Use of Happiness?

Let's look more closely at the cultural construction of happiness and at how mindfulness helped me to find my happiness in the above circumstance. According to Sara Ahmed, writer and scholar of feminist, queer, and race studies, in our society happiness is constructed in such a way that certain *objects* become attached to *happiness* and become desirable simply because we believe they will make us happy. Once an association between an object and the feeling we believe it will engender has been forged, I can even be happy in my *pursuit* of this thing because I have been led to believe it will make me happy.[3] The pursuit itself can brighten my world as I anticipate it will bring happiness, whether or not I actually end up experiencing happiness once the desired object is obtained (this may be why students rated themselves so highly on the MAAS score, simply anticipating that mindfulness will bring them more happiness).

Sometimes we really are not made authentically happy, or our life is not improved by the desired object. In that case, we may choose one of several options. Think about the things our society or culture says will bring you happiness: a perfect relationship, a particular job, fashion, wealth, health, a particular physique or physical appearance, and so on.

As a first option, we can simply choose to continue pursuing something that we've been led to believe will bring happiness, even if it never actually does. In the fashionable clothing example, we believe it will help us fit in or stand out in social circles. So, if we can afford it, we continue to purchase new clothing each season, discarding perfectly good clothing from past seasons, because we hope it will make us feel happier. Note there is no end to this chasing of happiness; it must be done every season from here into the future.

A second way we can respond is to adapt someone else's idea of happiness for our own, viewing it as more important than what might be best for us, in order to keep the peace and make others happy (or at least help them to avoid discomfort). Just for one example, persons of nondual sexuality may have experienced this for a time, at least early on in life.

---

3. Sara Ahmed calls this "anticipatory causality." Ahmed, *The Promise of Happiness*, 27–28.

A third alternative is that we can be happy for another person's happiness with this object, even though it doesn't make us happy. This is what I believe I chose, using mindfulness techniques, when engaged with the fashionable women. I found myself less judgmental and truly happy for them. In a sense, I achieved both a societal prescription for happiness (I could be happy for others) and a mindfulness promise of happiness as well (I experienced equanimity). But I did so without really questioning the wider happiness standards of our culture.

A fourth option is that we can take a stand; we can criticize the happiness object as false. We can expose the lie that its promise of happiness is universally applicable. In this case, we will be viewed as "outsiders" or "troublemakers." This is a difficult choice. Because the paradigm of happiness is so dominant, our criticisms may not ever be taken seriously by those choosing to go along with that paradigm. If we are labeled as a "troublemaker," we can be easily dismissed.[4]

Nearly a decade ago, my colleague Jay Kumar and I created a course entitled "Happiness: Exploring Its Spiritual and Rational Foundations," a course examining understandings of happiness in various world religions. It soon came to be known as the "Happiness Course" at our university. Since then, there have emerged a number of highly popular courses on happiness at other universities, as the topic has exploded in popularity. We begin our course by deconstructing cultural constructions of happiness prevalent in our society. We consider how a person or group who chooses not to go along with a particular happiness construct is essentially holding a mirror up to those who uphold the construct within the dominant society. Those who are harboring harmful cultural assumptions about what happiness is could look at their reflection in this mirror and take the opportunity for self-examination. They might then see that it is not that the outsider is wrong but that their own dominant concept of happiness

---

4. See chapter 2, "Feminist Killjoys," and chapter 3, "Unhappy Queers," in Ahmed, *The Promise of Happiness*.

is flawed. Yet, rather than peering into the mirror and facing what it reveals about their cultural assumptions, those holding the dominant, socially acceptable notion of happiness will more often find ways to discredit any who even slightly dare to suggest their concept of happiness may be harmful or delusional.

We can think of many examples of how this operates in society. If the happiness object is heterosexuality, it is common for hetero parents to worry for their children who may not be heterosexual, because they just want their child to be happy within society. They fear it will be a rough road for their child to continually move against the stream of the dominant culture. Queer, bisexual, and transgender individuals often stay in the closet for some time, in part in order to make heteronormative people feel comfortable.

The societally acceptable notion of happiness is further defended by invoking feelings of shame and guilt, reinforced through fear, in persons who challenge their culture's heteronormativity. This is enforced through actual violence, not just the fear of violence, in order to keep the happiness construct of heterosexuality intact. The very presence of a person who presents as gay, lesbian, or transgender threatens a fragile notion of happiness for some people. The threat to some people's notion of what their happiness consists of leads to violence against queer people every day in this country.

This means that bucking some happiness constructs, for example by a person identifying as nonbinary, can actually lead to their unhappiness because they are not accepted by the dominant society. This may be the case, but the fact that people often suffer for going against hegemonic norms in society ultimately means that the norms must be collectively challenged, not that we should focus primarily or only on teaching these persons adaptive strategies from the multiple self-help tools available (including mindfulness).

Mindfulness as a Happiness Object

Several years ago, I asked students in our "Happiness" course about happiness objects that they have been told, or that they themselves believe, will bring them happiness. They named the following: getting married, having children, finding an opposite-sex partner, moving out of their parents' home, having a stable career, and making lots of money. Today, they also mention doing meditation or mindfulness. In fact, I very often have students confess to me, "I know I should be doing mindfulness." What has happened is that *mindfulness* itself has become a *happiness object* in our culture. It is now an object people chase in order to find happiness, anticipating that it will make them happy. But as mindfulness is woven into the cultural construction of happiness today, what kind of happiness is it promising?

For one, as we have seen in my example about fashionable clothing, it promises the happiness of feeling comfortable in any circumstance, without having to examine the wider ethics of those circumstances in any way. Additionally, as a happiness object within culture, mindfulness becomes associated with particular characteristics defined by the dominant culture and market. Specific qualities begin to be associated with the happiness mindfulness brings, and are connected to certain types of people. We want to *be,* or at least to know, that person. We want what *they* have. Mindfulness is often represented by an "attractive" image that itself equals happiness—images like the young, beautiful, fit, sexy women on the cover of *Time* magazine issues on mindfulness.[5]

Or we may desire to be more like the mindfulness teacher who consistently exhibits traits of calmness, authenticity, and wisdom in front of his or her students. Personally, I have yet to sit with a teacher who displays dominant qualities other than these while they are teaching, although I have experienced in other settings their display of qualities that are not quite so attractive, like impatience and failing to listen. I very much include myself in this, as I reflect on some of my past teaching.

Certain character traits said to be developed through mindful-

---

5. See the following issues of *Time* magazine: August 4, 2003; February 3, 2014; and September 14, 2018.

ness, such as those mentioned above, have emerged as new social norms that are highly valued in the pursuit of happiness. Melvin Escobar, a teacher at East Bay Meditation Center in Oakland, California, suggests that this is a problem not only for mindfulness but also for American-style Buddhism. He says a monastic code favoring particular emotions has been overlaid on American Buddhism. There emerges a kind of attitude that if you don't meditate enough, if you aren't calm all the time, then you are not evolved. A type of spiritual bypass (i.e., demonstrating the *right* emotions—kindness, calm, acceptance, etc.) can corrupt mindfulness in our hyper-individualist society. This then leads to resentment of those who aren't being *mindful enough*—as though if only more individuals would just meditate, become conscious, and be calm, society would be better off.

But other kinds of emotions are needed in a healthy society, too. As Escobar asserts, for example, "Practitioners have a right to be angry."[6] He points out that certain qualities that are taught and favored over others by mindfulness teachers may in fact be "tools of the master,"[7] which serve the purpose of squashing the anger of those oppressed by race and gender-biased structural systems within our society.

Mindfulness: Awareness or Social Control?

Mindfulness can be helpful for regulating difficult emotions, as well as for developing awareness of one's own reactivity. This is particularly true in schools; the use of mindfulness with children has been shown to be very useful for improving attention, enhancing performance, regulating emotion, and alleviating feelings of anxiety and distress.[8] I am in no way denigrating the enormous benefits mindfulness can

---

6. Interview with Melvin Escobar, Turkish countryside, October 5, 2019.

7. Escobar, interview. He credits the concept of "the master's tools" to Audre Lorde, "The Master's Tools Will Never Dismantle the Master's House," in Audre Lorde, *Sister Outsider: Essays & Speeches* (Berkeley, CA: Crossing Press, 1984), 110–14.

8. "Why Mindfulness in Education," www.mindfulschools.org.

have as a tool to help children gain self-awareness and understand their own emotions.

What's concerning is the agenda behind the teaching. For instance, some suggest that mindfulness is being taught in schools in order to encourage students to accept rather than critically understand hardships in their lives, or to avoid acknowledging and tackling the socioeconomic factors that bring those hardships about. Mindfulness can help assure children stay calm and compliant even if they are in a school system that is designed to pressure them into increased productivity and higher assessment outcomes.[9]

Imagine if, instead, mindfulness was not marketed solely as a tool for procuring specific individual outcomes of self-awareness and control but *also* as a means of heightening the consciousness, particularly of older students, to the causes of racial or class disparity and privilege in American culture that give rise to unfair advantage. This is not a new idea. At the turn of this century, researchers suggested that mindfulness would be useful both in business and education for breaking up socially constructed notions of how we teach and considering what subjects are repeatedly taught without reflection on their social impact. The goal of this early movement of mindfulness into classrooms was not only to assist individuals with managing their emotions. It was aimed at discovering how increasing mindfulness could help to lessen social problems.[10]

More disturbing than the notion of mindfulness as social control in the classroom are the ways mindfulness has been purposely used by for-profit companies. In corporate America, mindfulness has developed into a tool for promoting social cohesion in service of capitalism. Mindfulness programs developed for corporate managers claim that mindfulness in the workplace introduces and circulates values

9. See Natalie Flores and Elisa Hartwig, "Here's Why You Need to Question Mindfulness in Classrooms," September 11, 2015, updated September 11, 2016, www.huffpost.com.

10. Ellen J. Langer and Mihnea Moldoveanu, "Mindfulness Research and the Future," *Journal of Social Issues* 56, no. 1 (2000): 129–39.

such as presence and self-mastery as managerial ideals. This in turn promotes an atmosphere of compliance in which everyone must fall in line in order to achieve the desired social cohesion. Bodies, emotions, and values are manipulated, chasing out certain kinds of people while those in agreement with dominantly defined mindful beliefs and identities remain secure in their jobs.[11]

In one study examining programs teaching mindfulness to employees, it was discovered that mindfulness can be an effective tool in the managerial toolbox but that it also has costs, or a "dark side." The researchers suggest that companies who are teaching mindfulness to their employees may not be getting the effects they desire, because some employees must engage in "surface acting" in order to do their jobs effectively.[12] That is, these employees have to hide their true feelings in order to do their job, such as placating a cranky customer or praising a product they wouldn't use themselves. As the researchers note, employees often cope by adopting a "mindless" approach when asked to complete such tasks, because "displaying inauthentic emotions takes work, and it often feels bad." They continue, "If [the employees] become more mindful, the unpleasant feelings that they had been suppressing (perhaps subconsciously) come to the fore. This in turn reduces job satisfaction and performance, as the mental resources needed for work get sapped by a newfound awareness of their own inauthenticity and negative emotions."[13]

---

11. Jaana Parviainen and Ilmari Kortelainen, "Becoming Fully Present in Your Body: Analysing Mindfulness as an Affective Investment in Tech Culture," *Somatechnics*, 9, nos. 2–3 (2019): 353–75, www.euppublishing. com/soma.

12. C. J. Lyddy, D. J. Good, M. C. Bolino, P. S. Thompson, and J. P. Stephens, "The Costs of Mindfulness at Work: The Moderating Role of Mindfulness in Surface Acting, Self-Control Depletion, and Performance Outcomes," *Journal of Applied Psychology* (2021), Advance online publication, https://doi.org/10.1037/apl0000863.

13. Christopher Lyddy, Darren J. Good, Mark C. Bolino, Phillip S. Thompson, and John Paul Stephens, "Where Mindfulness Falls Short," *Harvard Business Review*, March 18, 2021, https://hbr.org.

The researchers offer four strategies corporations might use to determine when the teaching of mindfulness might be beneficial. It's important to note that they do not suggest a change to the practice of having employees essentially lie on the job in order to increase production. Instead, the strategies they suggest for corporations include "targeting" the teaching of mindfulness, such as by not teaching it to employees who are required to engage in surface acting on the job. Second, they suggest paying attention to "timing"; for instance, a mindfulness break at the end of the day would be better than in the middle, "essentially offering more of a recovery exercise, instead of a real-time reminder of work stresses." Third, companies can offer distractions such as "fidget toys" so the employees don't get too emotional or anxious when they realize there is dissonance between their emotions and their required tasks at work. And finally, companies might cautiously consider strategies to encourage "deep acting," or getting employees to genuinely bring their values into alignment with those of the corporation.[14] The implication is that it would be preferable for companies to use the results of this study to manipulate uses of mindfulness, lest workers actually discover deeper benefits from mindfulness tools that might cause them to question what the company is requiring of them.

Corporations have created a new way to harness and manipulate the bodies and minds of workers in order to achieve greater productivity and profits. Indeed, if employees were taught introductory-level mindfulness exercises and then were offered the opportunity to delve more deeply into mindfulness practices, it's possible a worker could leave the company if they realize they are having to perform in ways that are inauthentic to their true feelings. They may even become a whistleblower if they observe unethical practices in the company. These are the outcomes the company fears. But other possibilities may also emerge: the employee could develop equanimity in observational reflection, becoming fully aware that their customers need

---

14. Lyddy et al., "Where Mindfulness Falls Short."

something other than what the worker is feeling inside and choose to have compassion both for themselves and for the customer. Living healthfully within this paradox is possible, but it is unlikely to result from a company-mandated mindfulness course.

We see clearly how mindfulness, as a happiness object, becomes a means to an end, or *purposive*. Such qualities as "guru attitudes" and "calculated compassion" are now prized among the managerial class. The introduction of "soft" mindfulness practices by managers to workers, meant to bring about a compassionate workplace, does not challenge the traditional "hard masculinity" of the managerial elite, who are utilizing the practices to enhance the workers' performance and productivity in a competitive marketplace. Researchers reviewing mindfulness managerial training for tech companies note that "the discourse of mindfulness is presented neutrally, emphasizing health and well-being and therefore avoids embarrassing and structural questions of class, race/ethnicity, and gender inequalities that also attend to some bodies and not others in the workplace."[15]

The purposes toward which mindfulness is being employed in some companies actually support the opposite of mindfulness proponents' claims that mindfulness will make us all happy, as these purposes instead reinforce white male corporate control under the guise of helping workers just to be more "present."

May You Be Happy

The most widely acclaimed use of mindfulness is that it will bring you happiness. Tens of thousands of books focus on happiness, including many books on mindfulness. Admittedly, many authors who couple mindfulness with happiness attempt to offer an alternative to popular societal understandings of happiness. But even though they may offer formulas for how mindfulness will bring happiness, very few of them actually define what happiness is. One exception to this is

---

15. Parviainen and Kortelainen, "Becoming Fully Present in Your Body," 370.

Matthieu Ricard, who has been deemed by the media to be the happiest man in the world.[16] In his book *Happiness: A Guide to Developing Life's Most Important Skill,* he submits that happiness involves "a deep sense of flourishing" that is related to a healthfully developed mind.[17]

Most books offering mindfulness as a pathway to happiness suggest that happiness is achievable through shifting your inner state; or it is possible through liberation from anxiety, fear, and anger; or that it is gained through developing a foundation of love, peace, and liberation within yourself.[18] They say happiness is related to calmness and peace of mind, and is stable and persistent. Happiness is achievable when you adopt an attitude of receptiveness that embraces life.[19] Real happiness results from the way you direct your attention, connecting to your own true experience, and then to others. Mindfulness teacher Sharon Salzberg contrasts this with "conventional happiness," which she characterizes as "the consolation of momentary distraction."[20] Some authors, such as Jay Kumar and Lexie Potamkin, acknowledge the importance of community in their explorations of self-awareness and happiness. Kumar writes of the centrality of "connection," "contribution," and "compassion" for happiness.[21]

What is interesting is not so much the definitions, or we might say

---

16. Alyson Shontell, "A 69–Year-Old Man Who Scientists Call the 'World's Happiest Man' Says the Secret to Being Happy Takes Just 15 Minutes a Day," *Insider,* January 27, 2016, https://www.businessinsider.com.

17. Matthieu Ricard, *Happiness: A Guide to Developing Life's Most Important Skill* (trans. Jesse Browner; New York: Little, Brown, 2003), 19.

18. Thich Nhat Hahn, *Happiness* (Berkeley, CA: Parallax Press, 2009), x–xi.

19. H. H. the Dalai Lama and Howard C. Cutler, *The Art of Happiness: A Handbook for Living* (New York: Riverhead Books, 1998), 25–26, 36.

20. Sharon Salzberg, *Real Happiness: The Power of Meditation* (New York: Workman Publishing, 2011), 198.

21. Jay Kumar, *Science of a Happy Brain: Thriving in the Age of Anger, Anxiety, and Addiction* (Conneault Lake, PA: Page Publishing, 2019); Lexie Brockway Potamkin, *Know Yourself: Develop a More Compassionate, Stronger, and Happier You* (Miami Beach, FL: What Is Peace, 2020).

the lack of actual definitions of happiness, but the repeated promises that mindfulness will bring true happiness. Even elusively defined, happiness is a popular and unquestioned value in our culture. Everybody wants to be happy!

For years I found it deeply uncomfortable to practice what has become known as *lovingkindness* meditations. These are practiced so often alongside classical mindfulness that many believe them to be foundational to mindfulness. I have heard many practitioners say they had trouble with them at first. I am not completely sure why I resisted them (a good psychoanalyst may be able to help us here!), but I can name two of the things that stood in my way. The first was their stilted language, which I later learned is taken straight from English translations of Eastern Buddhist chants and meditations. Second, I was not always ready to just be happy. In a lovingkindness meditation, you usually start by repeating a series of phrases directed toward various people and beings, in a certain order, such as: someone you love; yourself; someone you don't know well; someone you have difficulty with; your community; and all beings. The phrases might go something like this:

May you (I) be happy.
May you (I) be healthy in body and mind.
May you (I) be safe and protected from danger.
May you (I) be at peace.

Buddhists often call this *metta* meditation (a term now popular in mindfulness as well) and repeat the phrases in the form of ancient chants. Repeating them is believed to gradually open yourself to sense kind-heartedness toward all beings, including your enemies or those you have difficulty with. As I have learned more about the phrases, I have come to understand how repetition is designed to help open your heart to others over time. Yet, without much introduction, they felt to me for years as a compulsory requirement to be happy in order to be a good practitioner. When used in this way they can become just one more place where we encounter that elusive chase toward happiness.

The compulsory requirement of achieving happiness may just be one of the most effective tools utilized today toward the harnessing of mindfulness for social control. A company can ignore the enormous detrimental effects of their product on the environment if the product is advertised to make you happy. A tech company can hide the mining of the human mind and invasion of individual privacy built into the device they sell you in order to increase the company's revenue. They are successful in this subversion as long as they convince you they are offering a product guaranteed to make you happier. Corporate America convinces us it is our responsibility to increase our own happiness and that we will do so simply by purchasing their products.

Toward the end of *The Cancer Journals*, Audre Lorde, writing after her cancer diagnosis, questions the notion that our happiness should be our first responsibility, even amid illness. This emphasis on this individual obligation suggests that those who are not happy will somehow pay for it. She writes, "It is easier to demand happiness than to clean up the environment.... The happiest person in this country cannot help breathing in smokers' cigarette fumes, auto exhaust, and airborne chemical dust, nor avoid drinking the water, and eating the food."[22] Sara Ahmed submits that the very idea that I should be concerned for my happiness above all else should be met with communal, political resistance. She recalls Lorde's critique of happiness and suggests we must resist "the very idea that our first responsibility is for our own happiness." This means engaging in a political struggle against the prevalent ideology that happiness grows only from individual experience in a culture that fails to acknowledge structural causes of unhappiness.[23]

It is no coincidence that a multi-billion-dollar mindfulness industry has emerged at the same time as the rise of a culture that

---

22. Audre Lorde, *The Cancer Journals* (San Francisco, CA: Aunte Lute Books, 1997), 66–67, Kindle.
23. Ahmed, *The Promise of Happiness*, 83.

is obsessed with pursuing individual happiness. As theologian Joan Chittister notes in her book *Happiness*, over the last century humans began to study ourselves as individuals, to the point where "we have become our own objects of concern."[24] Mindfulness is marketed and taught as a way to be more comfortable with yourself and to be happy in the midst of any condition or circumstance, without noticing the structural inequalities giving rise to those conditions.

As a happiness object in and of itself, we need to consider seriously how mindfulness is robbed of the possibility of its use as a challenge to dominant cultural understandings of happiness. I submit that once a concept becomes a culturally accepted happiness object, its primary societal function becomes to support, rather than challenge, dominant constructs of happiness.

When a movement is benefiting so greatly from how well it fits into the market, it can be painful to recognize that the very happiness we seek contributes to unjust social systems that uphold the happiness of dominant, consumerist culture while keeping us, as a whole society, from achieving the happiness we so desire.

But, you may find yourself arguing, mindfulness helps millions of individuals to find relief from the experience of stress. Indeed, what mindfulness does quite well is help people cope with daily stress. The meditation practices themselves can help you find ways (if only for a few moments a day) to take time out and anchor yourself, at any given moment, with awareness of your body. The original purposes of the Mindfulness-Based Stress Reduction (MBSR) program, and today for many Mindfulness-Based Cognitive Therapy protocols (MBCT), are stress and pain reduction. These are invaluable tools in such an anxiety-ridden world.

And that is no small matter, according to even the most serious teachers. Mindfulness is marketed based on the premise that stress is not only a given and here to stay but it will inevitably increase—so

---

24. Joan Chittister, *Happiness* (Grand Rapids, MI: Eerdmans, 2011), 45.

we need solutions to help us find meaning in the midst of our stressful lives. The reason we all need to become mindful is because of the enormous and continually increasing stress we are all under.

But is this stress inevitable? Is it possible that, like happiness and mindfulness, stress too is culturally constructed? Again, definitions will get us only so far; so let's ask the question: How is stress being *used* in our culture? What purposes does it serve?

CHAPTER 4

What's the Use of Stress?

Stress clearly has a political use in helping us maintain a view of the individual as ill from society rather than acknowledging the need to tackle the ills of society.[1]

Several years before the pandemic began, I was honored to officiate at a wedding ceremony at the request of Clairre, a former student. Planning the wedding was a time of high emotion for her due to the strain of her job at the time. She was working for a company in which the demands of production and output kept her in a continual state of anxiety. Premarital counseling sessions with Clairre and her fiancé were fraught with her fear that the wedding might not go perfectly. These tensions were exacerbated by the daily anxiety of just balancing (or not) wedding planning and work. As it turned out, any fears Clairre had about family getting along or about the wedding not going smoothly did not turn out to be problems at all when the day finally arrived. After the wedding, Clairre soon came to a point of such stress at work that she could not continue; and because her spouse was able to work, she had the ability to quit, step out of the workforce, and reevaluate her priorities.

Two years later, Clairre contacted me to catch up on all that had been happening. She had just applied for her dream job, she said, and asked me to provide a work reference. She told me that the past year of

---

1. Dana Becker, *One Nation under Stress: The Trouble with Stress as an Idea* (New York: Oxford University Press, 2013), 75.

staying home full-time in a one-bedroom apartment (what they could afford on one income) during the COVID-19 pandemic had been difficult but a remarkable year for her and her new spouse. She commented that she and her partner are opposites; he is even-keeled and consistent, while Clairre is highly energetic. They complement one another and have found a routine—spending time together working out, eating healthy meals, and just enjoying one another's company. It has strengthened their relationship, she said. The coronavirus—an enormous shift in the conditions of their lives—offered the possibility of living more simply with less income, while providing them with the opportunity to drop many of the societal stressors of constant productivity.

Is stress inevitable? Forced into a new lifestyle by the pandemic, Clairre found out it was not. Yet we are reminded of stress at every turn today. Stress is popular. I Googled the term to get some idea of the enormity of its uses, and last time I checked got almost 21 billion results (the combination "stress and happiness" had 215 million hits; "stress and mindfulness" another 82 million). Stress is big, and mindfulness is now touted as one of the major antidotes to stress and as a magical elixir that will in turn bring you happiness!

The notion that centering in the present will alleviate your stress can be constructed as offering a false optimism, or as Lauren Berlant calls it, a "cruel optimism."[2] It can be cruel to offer hope that through simply learning to be more mindful as an individual you will find true happiness when the multiple and complex conditions making happiness unavailable to some of us due to conditions of deprivation and marginalization are left unaddressed.

I recently went back and listened to recordings of online courses, teacher talks, and advice given during mindfulness retreats I have attended, and I noticed a trend. One scenario is an example I have heard more than one variation on. It usually begins with a mindful-

---

2. Lauren Berlant, *Cruel Optimism* (Durham, NC: Duke University Press, 2011).

ness student asking the teacher for advice. The student shares they don't know how to handle the stress they experience when they come upon a mother yelling at her toddler in the grocery store. Implicit in the question is that the mother should not be showering her own anger upon her child, and the child is suffering as a result. Note the emphasis here is how the mindfulness student can cope when they experience stress upon observing someone else who is unable to manage their stress.

The teacher responds, first, by reminding the student to be mindful of their own emotions. Next, they suggest ways the student might calmly intervene to deescalate the situation. I even heard one teacher describe a time when they took it upon themselves to speak to a mother and offered her a compliment about her child. This created a moment in which the mother felt pride in her child. Success! The desired outcome was achieved, because for a few moments the mindful onlooker didn't have to feel stress upon witnessing what they perceived to be disturbing behavior in the mother.

The emphasis here is on how to deal with your own stress and judgment upon observing improper behavior. There is no awareness raised at all that in our society, it is overwhelmingly mothers who bear responsibility for the stress caused by their children's behaviors. Note that a mother is expected to regulate her own stressful emotions and reactions not just for herself. She is also responsible to do so in order to lessen the stress of others. It is her responsibility to make not only her own children but witnessing bystanders (even very mindful ones) feel better. Recall the compulsory desire built into society that each person has to pursue happiness. Mothers in our society are expected to follow this in order to make those around them comfortable. But I wonder if mindfulness can teach us to stop and examine the false, yet widely unquestioned, social construction of gender roles[3] that causes

---

3. Any role in society, such as that of a mother, is socially constructed and further defined depending on a multitude of factors that may include her race, class, or marital status.

enormous and unnecessary stress in some women's lives—and to see that the current construction of gender roles is a societal problem linked to upholding patriarchy and benefiting the economy.[4]

Stay with me—let's unpack some of the ways we view stress. As mindfulness teachers and marketers will remind you, Americans seem to be uniformly *stressed out*.

What Is Stress, Anyway?

Stress has not always been seen as something that must be continually managed. It used to be a term for occasional, specific difficulties that must be endured, more like a "storm-tossed ship" that needs to be skillfully maneuvered than a leaking boat that needs to be constantly bailed out. Dana Becker has coined the word "stressism" to refer to the current belief that many of the problems in contemporary life are primarily related to our individual lifestyles, and that the way they are solved is by each of us managing our own stress.[5] But the reality is that these individual life conditions are related to social conditions, whose solutions are in turn both political and social.

Stress today is understood as something we need to continually conquer as individuals. That may make sense on the surface, but just think about all the *objects* of stress—all the things we say are causes of stress. Start with aging. People have, with the exception of the fictional Benjamin Button, aged throughout their lifetimes in every time and culture. But in our culture today, the very act of getting older, and anything associated with it—wrinkles on your skin, different sleeping patterns, altered physical abilities, even facing one's death, all of which are part of a very natural process—are seen as stressors.

Issues related to health care, financial well-being, or social con-

---

4. In chapter 5 of *One Nation under Stress,* Becker offers an analysis of this issue, including the benefit to patriarchy and the economy of designating caregiving and the stress it entails as a problem that should be borne by individual women.

5. Becker, *One Nation under Stress,* 3–4, 18.

nections for older adults are also considered stressors for older members of society today. Yet, many of the burdens our aging population faces are not due to aging itself. They are due to economic, corporate, political, and societal structures that we have put into place (or not) that make obtaining proper nutrition, physical care, shelter, or basic health care difficult as one ages. We have developed many ways to cope with aging because we perceive it as a major stressor. For many, "successful aging" has come to mean to focus on the self by taking care of ourselves, using all the self-help tools available so that we can continue to be productive and develop a lasting legacy that enables us to live on long beyond our own physical life on earth.[6]

Society is witnessing enormous and increasing pressure in the form of an epidemic of loneliness, due to an ecosystem of political, economic, health factors that need to be tackled by society as a whole.[7] Because loneliness is particularly escalating among young people, we are doing what we can on university campuses by helping students to be ready to handle whatever comes their way, with resilience and reflective skills that will serve them in the future. These skills include spiritual and meditative practices as well as participation in groups with face-to-face dialogues. It also includes providing tech-free spaces in which to disconnect from continual distractions and online relationships, and empowering both interpersonal interaction and solitude, as needed.

Many causes of loneliness are out of a young person's control, including having lived through a pandemic where they were socially isolated from peers, facing looming debts, and dealing with health problems. The students, if they are facing such difficulties alone, perceive their sense of loneliness to be an individual problem. Yet many of the causes are societally induced. Their deep loneliness is fed by

---

6. Barbara Ehrenreich, *Natural Causes: An Epidemic of Wellness, the Certainty of Dying, and Our Illusion of Control* (New York: Hachette Book Group, 2018), 190, Kindle.

7. See Noreena Hertz, *The Lonely Century: How to Restore Human Connection in a World That's Pulling Apart* (New York: Currency, 2021).

such factors as FOMO, or fear of missing out, as they perceive everyone else on social media sites to be thriving. They may not have developed skills to make friends face-to-face, having spent the past years talking with their thumbs. This issue is exacerbated by technology companies' practice of developing ever-"smarter" devices designed to addict young people to their screens. And our culture is actually encouraging them to become even more dependent on their devices. If overuse of your phone is stressing you out, the answer, of course, is to download one more meditation or mindfulness app on it and use that to de-stress!

My colleague sent me a cartoon in which a woman was tied to a post with flames rising all around her. Another woman stood nearby, asking her, "Would you like to try a little yoga?" I sometimes feel that is what I am doing when I offer mindfulness to university professors. A young, tenure-track Black woman at a predominantly white university faces far more hurdles than many of her colleagues. She is often sought out by students for advice because they can relate to her, and she listens to them. She may go home from work each evening to care for a family. She may desire to study the incessant stressors placed by society on the lives of Black women, but the university may not consider her research to be on a serious enough topic. She will be asked to serve on many university committees to fill their diversity quota. All of her stressors are created by a system that privileges an ideal white male, who is granted the leeway to more readily choose whether or not to be accessible to students or serve on any committee, has no one depending solely on him for care, and is researching a traditional topic the academy deems worthy of his time. Yet, both will be expected to produce the same number of publications in order to be awarded tenure.

Women who choose a teaching track that is not tied to tenure, although they occupy a position just as integral to the university's ability to meet the needs of its students, are paid less and often sign contracts that stop during the summers and must be renewed each year. Throughout my university career, I have joined with women on task forces and committees tackling these issues, but in a system designed to privilege certain bodies over others, the status quo is slow to change.

The demands and stresses of any workplace are treated as if they are as natural as sagging skin as you age. And, because we see these as stresses borne by the individual, we have come to an agreement on the solution: it is up to everyone to manage, overcome, and solve stress in his or her life. Conveniently, mindfulness has emerged as a billion-dollar industry that offers adaptive self-help strategies, upholding the fantasy of inevitable and increasing stress best solved by individuals working on themselves.

But when stress is seen as an individual problem to be solved, it leaves unchallenged the unjust social, economic, and political factors that undergird that stress. Societal causes are either ignored or explained away as a product of individual thinking, and thus easily dealt with through individual means.

Who's Got the Most Stress?

Because our culture tends to see stress as a personal problem to be solved, everyone is assumed to be under equal amounts of stress. And if one of the solutions you have before you is to do some mindfulness practices, for example, it follows that everyone needs mindfulness, all the time.

Hence, people incarcerated in prison need mindfulness, but so do CEOs of Fortune 500 companies. It has been argued that the latter may even need it more, because their suffering can cause the suffering of thousands of people they influence,[8] as they face the enormous demands of constantly increasing productivity and competition as an unquestioned good. But keep in mind that a percentage of prisoners in our nation are falsely imprisoned and more are incarcerated

---

8. Max Zahn, "'Even the Rich Suffer': An Interview with Google's Jolly Good Fellow Chade-Meng Tan," https://religiondispatches.org, April 26, 2016.

because of class and racial profiling, having committed crimes equal to those of white, privileged people not living behind bars. In the world of mindfulness that ignores the social causes of the pressure cookers the prisoner and CEO respectively live in, they are perceived to suffer not only equally, but equally inevitably.

Just glance at ads for adaptive and self-help strategies. You'll find that the stressors named include a wide range of items with completely different societal causes: illness, organizing a party, losing a job, remodeling a house, grieving a loved one, bullying, racial discrimination, workplace deadlines, spousal abuse, and living in poverty, to name a few. As Dana Becker notes, "Poverty cannot be equated with wedding preparations or even chronically stressful work situations; it is a set of *conditions* that brings with it high-crime neighborhoods, poor schools, and, for some, compromised social networks."[9]

To imagine that stress is the same for everyone and is just made up in our heads is not only cruel, it is also an assumption that could only be made by the privileged, as a solution in a structure where there are deep divides between those gaining from capitalist productivity and those falling behind. The stress I feel when witnessing a woman yelling at her child in the grocery store likely pales in comparison with the stresses she faces, which might include educational challenges and a lack of resources for the child, work pressures, joblessness, lack of support or abuse from a partner, or any number of social or economic hurdles.

Alleviating Stress with Gratitude

Just be grateful for your child, some of us might want to say to the mother. A new industry that is being woven into self-help and many mindfulness offerings is emerging: the gratitude industry. You are now encouraged at every turn to just show some gratitude, and you will gain ease in your life. Studies are said to show that if you only stop and be grateful for what you have, and if you regularly count

---

9. Becker, *One Nation under Stress,* 92.

your blessings, you will feel more optimistic about your life and will be happier.[10] Gratitude is peddled, often by well-meaning people, within a culture wherein Americans are primarily consumers, not citizens. In this milieu, gratitude for those things you feel you have earned or been lucky enough to receive fits beautifully. Once again, we find a tool with which we can manage all our stresses on our own, and it follows that everyone else should be able to do the same. Gratitude has been dubbed a new "religion"[11] and a "privatized spirituality of success"[12] by those who deconstruct the individualist nature it has taken on and who thus try to explore its more spiritual side.

Filling your life with gratitude journals, rocks, collages, thoughts, jars, prompts, or meditations may help your mood or outlook. But it can also very easily overlook or even be complicit in injustice and ignore the pain of others.[13] We've discussed how the world does not change solely because individuals feel grateful or personally happy. Peddling gratitude, a favorite theme in much mindfulness marketing, can easily be another tactic to convince people who are marginalized to solve it themselves: just be grateful for what you have. It follows that those with the most can be grateful for all their fortune, whether they perceive it as good luck or as having pulled themselves up by their bootstraps. The language of gratitude as the language of luck or of self-achievement ignores all the socio-economic-racist-sexist-homophobic factors that go into creating a system wherein certain people get lucky or have more opportunities to excel so much more often than others.

---

10. "Giving Thanks Can Make You Happier" *Harvard Health*, November 22, 2011, https://www.health.harvard.edu.

11. Lillian Daniel, *When "Spiritual but Not Religious" Is Not Enough: Seeing God in Surprising Places, Even the Church* (New York: Jericho Books, 2013), 9.

12. Diana Butler Bass, *Grateful: The Subversive Practice of Giving Thanks* (New York: HarperOne, 2018), xxi, Kindle.

13. Bass, *Grateful*, 185; see also chapter 8, "Circles of Gratitude."

The rhetoric of gratitude is too often a rhetoric of debt in our culture—someone does something for me, and I owe them something (at the least, a thank-you). In this schema, one can easily feel gratitude while feeling indifferent to others. A far too obvious example occurred when the richest man in the world, Jeff Bezos, thanked his Amazon employees (who have been shown to be underpaid and exploited) and his millions of customers for paying for his joyride to the edge of space and back, following the inaugural launch of his Blue Origin spacecraft.[14] "The rhetoric of the debt of gratitude has become one of the most effective techniques of power in the contemporary world," writes Jeremy David Engels.[15]

So what would a more spiritual, less individually focused, attitude of gratitude entail?

It entails resistance, for one. Diana Butler Bass points out that even if we are among the people who live more gratefully, we can be compared to fish swimming in water that has been polluted. Gratitude and resistance come together when we band together to clean up the river rather than offer thanks for our position in the river. We forget how easily we have become used to its toxicity, which will undo our health in the long run.[16]

We can resist the idea that gratitude simply means personal acceptance and thanks, and that we should all just feel grateful for what we have. When NFL football players began to "take a knee" during the playing of the national anthem, they were accused of ingratitude for the country, our military, and for their own large salaries. Yet, they could also be understood as resisting the idea that we celebrate a

---

14. See "Bezos Thanks Amazon Workers and Customers for His Vast Wealth, Prompting Backlash," *New York Times*, July 20, 2021, https://www.nytimes.com; and Michael Sainato, "'I'm Not a Robot': Amazon Workers Condemn Unsafe, Grueling Conditions at Warehouse," *The Guardian*, February 15, 2020, https://www.the guardian.com.

15. Jeremy David Engels, *The Art of Gratitude* (New York: SUNY Press, 2018), loc. 1009 of 5915, Kindle.

16. Bass, *Grateful*, 165.

country that does not live up to its ideals. Or resisting the notion that in a country called the "land of the free," Black people are daily targeted and killed in far greater proportions than people of other races.

Gratitude can mean thanks for abundance that is or could be shared by all, attained through political struggle. Engels suggests using instead the term "gratefulness," which he defines as "the emotional experience of being moved by thanksgiving for life."[17] This is thanksgiving for what we share: aliveness itself, including life this very day on this very earth. It is recognition that all life matters and does not take for granted the lives of some over others. Gratefulness is thanksgiving for abundance, not just for what is "mine."

It is deeply unfortunate that gratitude has been exploited by ideologies upholding systems of power in place, just as the harnessing of mindfulness has been. This exploitation trivializes the importance and beauty of gratefulness as a response to life itself—all of life abundant, within and around us.

Is Stress Inevitable?

We can agree that in some degree or another for many in our culture stress is real. But what about the claim of self-help peddlers that it is inevitably increasing? Throughout the first two months of stay-at-home orders under the threat of COVID-19, in my role as university dean of the chapel, I had many conversations with students, faculty, and staff, and came to believe that in the face of the pandemic, almost everyone in America was experiencing grief—over the loss of their daily routine, job, income, contact with people, health, or even the death of their loved ones.

As COVID-19 swept across the world and the United States, people felt increasingly under pressure. Workers and students suddenly had to leave businesses and schools; ordered to stay-at-home for their own safety, many family members were living in cramped conditions or abusive circumstances that were not safe at all. Some parents

---

17. Engels, *The Art of Gratitude,* loc. 2821 of 5915.

had lost even the funds needed to feed their families. High school and college graduations were postponed. Wedding and travel plans were thwarted. People were prevented from sitting at the bedside of an ill or dying relative for fear of catching the virus themselves.

Mindfulness was suddenly in enormous demand. My colleagues and I had increasing requests for online mindfulness sessions and webinars on stress relief. I was able to witness firsthand how well mindfulness and similar techniques really worked to deal with daily pressures in the midst of a global crisis. We all needed to cope with the trauma caused by the pandemic, which was affecting every home in various ways. During this time, mindful presence and a measured perspective undoubtedly helped many people.

This brought good news for the blossoming mindfulness movement. People who were seeking ways to live in unasked-for circumstances, with stressors they never before imagined, turned to the internet. To their credit, those mindfulness teachers who had accumulated enormous followings—many of whom had achieved wealth through teaching fees and voluminous book sales—turned quickly (one could say mindfully) to releasing resources and offering classes online, often free of charge. Seeing the desperate need for stress relief, they jumped into action from their own couches and home offices. The demand was up, and it was being met. Companies like Ten Percent Happier offered their meditation app free to teachers and other key workers during the pandemic. The extraordinary circumstances of the pandemic prompted an outpouring of compassion. Yet, was it enough or sustainable in a society normally predicated on constant production and increased pressure on individuals and communities?

The experience of many during the pandemic confirmed that increases in the commercial success of the mindfulness industry are tied to continual and increasing stress in people's lives. While previously this stress was often caused by a capitalist urgency for progress, such as in the workplace, during the pandemic stress was caused by a halt in that continual production, with many finding themselves with little or no safety net to fall back upon.

But living through the pandemic also confirmed an opposite possibility—that increasing stress may not be inevitable. Some people discovered that the stress in their lives was actually reduced when they slowed down, as we saw with Clairre. Parents spent less time commuting and more time with their children. Shopping time was minimized as it shifted online. The constant consumption of nonessential goods was cut in half for most people, even those with disposable income. According to some surveys, Americans spent stimulus payments on committed expenses and, if possible, savings and investments—not entertainment or elective purchases.[18] For many, life was simplified.

Additionally, as human consumption slowed, the earth and the environment breathed a sigh of relief. Stars were seen over Los Angeles, and ocean islands were more clearly visible from the shore. People took evening walks to breathe in clearer air and gazed in wonder at videos of emerging animal life and foliage. Those purchases people were able to make included kayaks, bikes, and hiking boots for venturing into the outdoors. Continual and increased production, with its accompanying pollution, consumption, and resulting stress, may not be inevitable after all, it turns out.

World renowned climatologist Hesham El-Askary works with Earth Systems Science Data Solutions lab (EssDs) scientists who monitored atmospheric emissions and their relation to how different countries responded to the COVID-19 pandemic. I asked him whether any lessons for our relationship with the earth were emerging from their research.

El-Askary explained that we have witnessed and lived through a changing climate with irreversible consequences, the global temperature rising on average by 1 degree Celsius. The year 2020 was seen as a crucial one for action toward keeping our temperature increase to less than 1.5 degrees Celsius by 2030, even before we knew that it would be the year of COVID. Throughout the pandemic, El-Askary and

---

18. "Envestnet/Yodlee COVID-19 Income and Employment Trends," Envestnet/Yodlee, https://www.yodlee.com.

other scientific observers carefully measured how globally enforced social distancing measures (such as stay-at-home mandates, making remote schooling and working a necessity) dramatically contributed to massive drops in atmospheric pollution.

The message we can take from this, El-Askary urges, is to learn from our mistakes and take what is going on as an opportunity to continue along this new positive trajectory rather than return to our usual ways. If we do not shift our practices that are contributing to climate change, according to El-Askary, we will increasingly be prone to an increase in the frequency and magnitude of natural weather disturbances, or "anomalous behavior of natural events" that are climate driven.[19] This will affect some nations more than others but will be felt worldwide. In the United States we are currently experiencing massive wildfires, as are other parts of the world. As we lose forest cover through wildfires, we lose the main source that captures carbon dioxide in the atmosphere; at the same time, increasing industrial conditions increase carbon dioxide, affecting the proper balance of our ecosystems. Higher temperatures are contributing to the loss of snow cover in the mountains, which contributes to a rise in temperature of the oceans, thus affecting sea life and the biodiversity of ocean habitats.

This increase in natural disasters will cause a "domino effect" or "positive feedback effect" so that it is difficult to know which phenomenon is causing which effect that is stressing the atmosphere and biosphere.[20] It will become a chicken-and-egg problem. The result of this spiral of effects is that more lives will be lost and economies will be negatively affected. El-Askary believes the pandemic offered all of us a collective opportunity to think deeply about our behavior and to commit to making positive impacts to ensure new life for the future of the earth and all beings on the earth.[21]

---

19. Hesham El-Askary, conversation with author, September 11, 2020.
20. Hesham El-Askary, conversation with author, September 11, 2020.
21. Hesham El-Askary, interview by author, April 6, 2020. I first

Postpandemic recovery efforts could also bring awareness to the ways the environmental crisis intersects with poverty, health care, and food insecurity, as it is the poorest neighborhoods that often suffer the most from environmental damage, just as they suffered the greatest losses during the pandemic. It turns out that our constant and continual production is heavily contributing to the stress of the earth and its inhabitants. Part of lessening our stress is shifting the conditions in which we live, not just trying to reduce it on our own through mindfulness exercises.

Stress, it turns out, may not have to be inevitably increasing. Nor does everyone everywhere experience stress equally. Stress is largely societally induced, but the construction of stress in commerce and in the media convinces us that it is our responsibility to "solve" its rapidly increasing hold on our lives.

Yet, you might argue, at least mindfulness helps people deal with their individual, personal emotions. Don't all people experience stressful emotions the same way? We turn next to ask whether emotions are individual, or whether there is a way in which they are born of and borne by the collective, just as stress is. We examine the nature of emotion and its relationship to social constructions, particularly of gender and race. What's the use of emotion?

---

reported this interview in a blog, "Earth Day, Ridván, and Ramadan: Socially Distant yet Inspiring Action," April 15, 2020, https://blogs.chapman.edu/fish.

Chapter 5

Emotion: Gendered and Racialized

Shame as a circulated emotion . . . sticks to some bodies more than others, especially bodies that transgress social norms, whether those are norms of gendered behavior, heterosexual orientations, or racial suppositions.[1]

Collective Emotion

I vividly recall the day Christine Blasey Ford testified before a Senate judiciary hearing when Brett Kavanaugh was being considered for a seat on the bench of the Supreme Court of the United States. Ford accused Kavanaugh of sexually assaulting her when they were in high school. For four hours, she recounted the assault in vivid detail. As the country halted and millions listened to her testimony, women across the country relived violent acts they had encountered. My body shuddered and my emotions contracted as I re-experienced the helplessness I felt at a moment when I was detained and rendered powerless by a system of male power. I recalled every sinister comment throughout my professional career (some quite recently) by male colleagues emotionally establishing their superiority over me, each time leaving me feeling violated.

That day reopened the floodgates of the #metoo movement, a term first coined by Tarana Burke in 2006. Burke talks about hearing a young girl's story of horrible sexual abuse by her mother's boy-

---

1. Jeana Moody, "Feeling through Language: Tracing Affect in Gendered Language" (MA thesis, Oregon State University, May 31, 2019), 44.

friend, and being unable to listen or respond to her at the time. She writes,

> I just watched her walk away from me, visibly struggling to recapture those secrets and tuck them back into their hiding place. I watched her put her "mask" back on her face and return to the world. And as I stood there, I couldn't even bring myself to whisper the words circling my mind and soul: "Me too."[2]

Countless women live with violence every day, and with fear that has pulsed throughout history and has been revisited by generations of women. The trauma I felt was mine, but it was also ours; millions of women across the country felt it, continuing the trauma of our grandmothers and great-grandmothers whose minds as well as bodies were violated under patriarchal systems perpetuating violence against women.

The Kavanaugh hearing occurred the day before my long-term, long-distance partner had a heart attack. Soon after, it appeared he was going to recover, and I was preparing to visit him. I called the Sunday morning prior to my flight that week, to hear Ron's son answer his cell phone with the words, "Dad died last night." Ron had collapsed again and died of heart failure.

I fell to the floor, my heart screaming along with my voice. My lungs heaved, gasping for breath. My whole body shook with guilt (I wasn't there) and numbness as I looked to the future without him (we talked of retiring together). For months on end the future was simply a fog as I first slogged and eventually walked through each day, literally feeling as though my heart was folded in half. Over the next few years, with the support of family members and close friends, I felt my heart slowly begin to open again.

I have known debilitating experiences of feeling violated, perpetrated by sexism. I have experienced the searing pain of

---

2. Tarana Burke, "History and Inception," metoo, https://metoo mvmt.org.

personal grief. And I also see the way we suffer as a society from collective grief.

COVID-19 and Black Lives Matter

The invasion of COVID-19 and the eruption of Black Lives Matter in the spring of 2020 revealed the unequal pain and stress due to enormous racial and gender disparities in the United States, and the violence engendered by police brutality, poverty, and unequal access to health care and basic human rights.

The experience of women when stay-at-home orders hit during COVID-19 confirmed how the subordinate treatment of women, whose minds are undervalued and bodies continually violated, is systematically embedded in society. It reaffirmed that women are expected to be the caring ones, while men are excused from similar emotions and duties. With children at home to care for, full-time working mothers of young children lost 2.2 million jobs between February and August 2020 alone, three times the rate of full-time fathers.[3]

These statistics are multiplied when looking specifically at women of color. As one protestor put it, the country saw the reality that for Black and Brown people, living in this country means living in a constant state of mourning. The pandemic magnified for all to see the unmistakable statistics showing that Black, Native American, and Latinx members of our society would disproportionately die of COVID-19. These deaths were associated with systematic injustices, such as when populations continuing to perform essential work in unsafe conditions simultaneously lacked access to basic nutrition, health care, and education. According to CDC data, Black and Amer-

---

3. Tim Henderson, "Mothers Are 3 Times More Likely than Fathers to Have Lost Jobs in Pandemic," *PEW*, September, 28, 2020, https://www.pewtrusts.org; see also Nicole Bateman and Martha Ross, "Why Has COVID-19 Been Especially Harmful for Working Women?" *Brookings*, October, 2020, https://www.brookings.edu.

ican Indian or Alaska Native persons had a rate approximately four times, and Hispanic or Latinx persons approximately three times, that of white persons for hospitalization due to severe COVID-19 symptoms.[4]

When the video capturing the murder of George Floyd by a white police officer swept the airwaves,[5] millions of Americans took to the streets to protest not only Floyd's murder but also the unnecessary and unrelenting pain and grief collectively visited on the Black community in this country. Floyd's murder shed light on the dozens and dozens of recent and historic deaths of Black people targeted as dangerous and often killed by police, ostensibly because they appeared to be a threat. And as my colleague Shaykh Jibreel Speight noted in June 2020:

> A system exists wherein certain people . . . exert their power and will on others who were, count with me, please: driving, jogging, sleeping, yelling, parking, selling CDs, selling cigarettes, walking at night, carrying a phone, wearing a hoodie while carrying Skittles, babysitting, opening the door, holding a toy gun, being homeless, having a broken taillight, exercising, shopping at Walmart, eating ice cream, grilling, or even birdwatching. Twenty! And that's just the minimum.[6]

The simple privilege of walking the streets without fear of being killed because your blackness is the first thing some police or white civilians see and react violently to is a stress and a fear not experienced by all Americans.

---

4. "Disparities in COVID-19 Associated Hospitalizations," Centers for Disease Control and Prevention (CDC), https://www.cdc.gov.

5. Derek Chauvin dug his knee into Floyd's neck for nearly ten minutes, even after he had become unresponsive. See Eric Levenson, "Former Officer Knelt on George Floyd for 9 Minutes and 29 Seconds—Not the Infamous 8:46," *CNN*, March 30, 2021, www.cnn.com.

6. Jibreel Speight, "Words of Reflection from Vigil for Victims of Racism and Call to Action," June 12, 2020, https://blogs.chapman.edu/fish.

In the weeks following the murder of George Floyd, Marionette Oliver, cochair of a church committee I also sit on, happened to be scheduled to offer the opening reflection for our monthly online meeting. It was the first time she had shared her story with the rest of us on the committee. She and her family are African American, and she told us she and her husband moved to Orange County, California, from Macon, Georgia, years ago when her children were still young, into a neighborhood that is still 95 percent white. Marionette said she worries the same way she did the day she moved in.

> I worry every time my sons leave home. My oldest son lives in Portland with his wife and children. He calls me two to three times each week when walking his dog. I worry. Our youngest son lives with us. When he goes out to run or ride his bike, I worry. Don, my husband, is now retired. When we don't go out together, I worry. Living in a community where the majority of people don't look like me, I worry every day.[7]

Marionette has since shared with me that her worries have intensified in recent years as a result of the increasingly divisive political climate in our country.

Tracking Emotion

Who gets to be fully happy in our culture? What if tracking the history of emotion, just as with tracking the history of happiness, tracks the history of its distribution? There is a connection between the emergence of individuals with particular dominant emotions and the ways in which they align with the collective. Dominant emotions can vary and be influenced by the historic and present-day conditions of a person's life, such as whether one is primarily oppressed or privileged within the socioeconomic system.[8]

---

7. Marionette Oliver, Committee on Ministry of the Presbytery of Los Ranchos meeting, June 4, 2019.

8. See Sara Ahmed, *The Cultural Politics of Emotion* (New York: Routledge, 2015), 71.

While emotional trauma is experienced by individuals, many today agree it is also a shared experience. Perpetuated by systematic racist and sexist policies, trauma is embedded in our DNA and spans generations. If we want to address emotions with mindfulness, we must be cognizant of how they are shaped by generations of policies and practices.[9]

Think about dominant emotions and who is said to have which ones or, more accurately, is allowed to display them. By observing the language of commentators regarding a female or a Black man running for office versus a white male, we can see how the same emotions, when displayed by different people, can be either celebrated or scorned. If Hillary Clinton made an angry comment when she was running for president, she was dismissed by some as unfeminine, emotional, and a bitch. If Donald Trump showed anger, he was hailed as a hero who stood up for what he believed. When Barack Obama displayed anger, he was criticized and feared as an angry Black man and accused of not being a true American.

Emotions are allowed or not for certain bodies, but specific emotions are also placed on, and become attached to, certain bodies. This has been true for persons taking (or not) their proper place in a gendered hierarchy within society. Jeana Moody argues that language around emotion shapes our cultural space and a sense of belonging or unbelonging for both masculine and feminine roles. Fear of violence, or of not being perceived as normal within an assigned binary gender, maintains that space. She writes, "Fear as a socially and linguistically circulated emotion sticks to some bodies, defining them as out-of-place, expanding on histories of violence against particular communities. Fear comes up again and again as a reaction to public harassment and shapes bodies in public space as belonging, safe,

---

9. See Resmaa Menakem, *My Grandmother's Hands: Racialized Trauma and the Pathway to Mending Our Hearts and Bodies* (Las Vegas, NV: Central Recovery Press, 2017), 9–10, Kindle.

comfortable, or unbelonging, at risk, and uncomfortable."[10] Certain emotions circulate through the population and become attached to those who transgress expected racial and gendered norms.

Mindfulness Claims

Many claim that mindfulness practice will bring about self-compassion, which will, in turn, lead to compassion toward others, ultimately leading to a more compassionate society. While developing empathy is critical, we cannot assume that means that we understand the deepest pain another person experiences, such as the pain comingled with anger and betrayal by a society built on white supremacy, unless we are the target of that bigotry. Or the real fear of violence within a patriarchal system that shames our gender and/or gender identity. What we can do is choose to walk alongside those who experience these kinds of suffering and to act to alleviate the societal constructions that bring about the circumstances leading some to such depths of pain.

Many mindfulness teachers are, thankfully, introducing greater understanding of the way society shapes emotions. Rhonda Magee writes that compassion is essential as a foundation for mindfulness. For her, compassion is not just taking the perspective of others, like having empathy, or feeling sorry for those whose lives may be less fortunate than our own, or like having pity. Compassion is not a feeling. Instead, she defines compassion as "the will to act to alleviate the suffering of others."[11]

Teachers are emphasizing that, while mindful settling in your body is individual work, it must be grounded within the context of interconnected cultural work. Resmaa Menakem writes separately to white people, Black people, and police officers. He suggests that the

---

10. Jeana Moody, "Feeling through Language," 43.

11. Rhonda V. Magee, *The Inner Work of Racial Justice: Healing Ourselves and Transforming Our Communities through Mindfulness* (New York: TarcherPerigree, 2019), 32, Kindle.

discovery of deep cultural histories and context begins with mindfully centering in the body. He clarifies this to mean specific bodies—bodies that are themselves embedded in particular social, racialized communities, bodies with particular shared pain, unexamined blind spots, and collective histories. Pointing out that ours is a culture of white-body supremacy that has been building for centuries, Menakem asserts:

> This means that no matter what we look like, if we were born and raised in America, white-body supremacy and our adaptations to it are in our blood. Our very bodies house the unhealed dissonance and trauma of our ancestors.
>
> *This* is why white-body supremacy continues to persist in America, and why so many African Americans continue to die from it.[12]

He describes trauma as culture forming and contagious, passed along by patriarchy and structural racism. It lives in our bodies, so that lives are changed when culture is changed. Menakem describes the need for causing inflammation in the culture, just as inflammation is a naturally protective response of the body to injury and is at times necessary in order to heal. This disruptive healing occurs through social activism that wisely creates needed disruptions in culture. It is needed for the collective Black body and the collective American body in order to help the culture heal.[13]

Embedding Mindfulness in Justice Making

Concern about race and gender inequality has recently been flooding mindfulness teacher websites. Yet, individuals who have been or are currently in training with top mindfulness teachers are having to discover for themselves ways to incorporate awareness of patriarchal, white-body supremacy into mindfulness practice. While writing this

---

12. Menakem, *My Grandmother's Hands,* 10.
13. Menakem, *My Grandmother's Hands*, 257–58.

section, I serendipitously met and had the opportunity to interview three remarkable men, each of whom brought wisdom to my understanding.

Terrence

Terrence is established in his professional career, into which he has been incorporating mindfulness for some years. As a Black man, he thought it especially important to have a teacher certification in order to be taken seriously in this work. Terrence shared that the emphasis on diversity in the application process for a prominent mindfulness program led him to believe that race would be a central lens for mindfulness liberation in this teacher-training course. He quite soon discovered, however, that it was more of a decorative diversity; it turned out to be one more program intentionally attracting BIPOC (Black, Indigenous, and people of color) participants, just to appear diverse. At least one other Black participant in the program, he found, enrolled for the same reason he did; they felt they needed validation by a white mindfulness establishment.

The core program and its values, he soon noticed, are geared to the individual bourgeois white subject. Required retreats assume one can take time off from daily responsibilities, either to achieve total silence in one's own home to participate online or to afford to fly to a retreat center across the country. Such expectations are imbued with basic assumptions of accessibility and privilege. Beyond that, a deep emphasis on isolated individual practice assumes one can separate from the conditions of one's community or culture, and that suffering can be alleviated solely by learning this individual mindful practice.

Terrence was taken aback when he heard the primary ethical dilemma voiced by many of his cohorts in the mindfulness teaching program, which was mainly comprised of what he described as older white women who saw themselves as nonreligious. Perceiving mindfulness as rooted in Buddhism and seeing Buddhism as a religion, their primary question was whether practicing mindfulness makes them Buddhist, and whether they can separate their practice from any religion.[14]

Terrence notes that when a teacher-training program has been largely geared toward a bourgeois white, mainly female subject, it's likely that its primary purpose is personal growth. I would also point out that these individual white subjects, especially older white women with the resources to fully participate as the main subjects of mindfulness programs (which includes me), are culturally privileged in American society. We are, for example, able to make individual decisions to separate from culture and community and focus on self-improvement. We are more likely to be in an economic and social position to have the luxury to choose whether or not to live alone in quiet; or to eat only expensive, fresh vegan diets; or to have adequate alternative social support so we can easily declare that we have no need for a religious community.

Resmaa Menakem reminds us that culture "is how our bodies retain and reenact history—through the foods we eat (or refuse to eat); the stories we tell; the things that hold meaning for us; the images that move us; what we are able (and unable) to sense or feel or process; the way we see the world; and a thousand other aspects of life."[15]

What Terrence points out is profound—that there is a culturally based aspect of mindfulness, both in the ways it is taught and marketed and in the ways it is internalized by participants from different cultures. He reflects, "I think of myself as working with Black knowledge-based mindfulness, because I'm reaching toward the African roots of Black humanity."[16]

After some time reviewing the mindfulness teacher program and its objectives and populist notions of mindfulness, Terrence observes, "As someone Black and Queer I am asking specific questions around

---

14. Terrence (pseudonym), interview by author, February 10, 2021.
15. Menakem, *My Grandmother's Hands*, 245.
16. Terrence, interview.

trauma and healing in the service of a different liberation project than what is being asked by the mindfulness industry."[17] The question arises again in my mind: Can mindfulness, as it is being envisioned and taught today, be liberatory for particular communities that have experienced serious trauma and are seeking healing?

Justice

For Justice Crudup, mindfulness underlies his commitment to compassionate activism against racial bias. He began meditating in high school, when he was struggling with his identity and place in the world, and later took up a serious practice of meditation in college. Justice then explored various mindfulness and Buddhist meditation centers throughout the Los Angeles area after graduation. He finally felt genuinely welcomed at the Hsi Lai Temple, one of the largest Buddhist temples in North America, practicing a form of Buddhism that originated in Taiwan. He accepted the Buddhist ethical precepts for living his life in a formal ceremony, taking refuge in the Triple Gem, and continues to participate in the community today.

Justice attributes fully coming into his own identity, embracing all the aspects of what it means to be Black in America, to his meditation, which has been a long journey of inward reflection and outward ethical responsibility. He acknowledges that coming to understand that "our thoughts are not our thoughts" was, for him, "where the deeper work begins." He laments however, that "a lot of people don't want to do the deeper work, but that's where it really begins."[18] Justice is working with young people in the Black Lives Matter movement to help promote awareness of the ways they can contribute not only to protest but to real changes, both within themselves and in society.[19]

---

17. Terrence, email correspondence with author, September 12, 2021.
18. Justice Crudup, interview by author, March 31, 2021.
19. See more on the work of Justice Crudup in chapter 6.

Justin

One young man's mindfulness teaching, connected to awareness of racialized and gendered issues, has begun reaching thousands of young people. Justin Michael Williams began meditating in college, at the age of twenty. He recalls that he was one of the "only ones" learning meditation in his community, in many ways: one of the only men, one of the only queer people, one of the only Black people, one of the only young people.

A decade later, his book, *Stay Woke*, emerged. In it, Williams asserts that it is crucial for people to become awake to obstacles in their lives through meditation, such as traditions that are outdated or that cause you to doubt yourself and continually seek validation from other people. But he believes that we need to understand something first: although your thoughts do influence reality, he says, "Your thoughts don't create your reality."[20] Reality is co-created. Trauma, for example, is carried in the culture, not just in the mind. He writes:

> Your thoughts don't create your reality when you live in the South Bronx and suffer from the highest levels of asthma in the United States, affecting your health and wellbeing for the rest of your life, or when you live in Flint, Michigan, and your brain is damaged by poisoned water that your country won't do anything about. Your thoughts don't create your reality when you're a little girl who is molested by her stepfather before the age of six. Your thoughts don't create your reality when you're a young black boy who gets shot walking down the street just because you're wearing a hoodie. Thoughts didn't create the reality of the victims of 9/11, refugees seeking asylum, children slain in school shootings, black trans women who are disproportionately impacted by hate crimes and fatal violence, Native people whose lands have been stolen, or the millions of people around the world overcoming sexism, racism, oppression, genocide,

---

20. Justin Michael Williams, *Stay Woke: A Meditation Guide for the Rest of Us* (Boulder, CO: Sounds True, 2020), 32, Kindle.

environmental ruin, homophobia, xenophobia, stress inequity, or (insert the injustice of your choice here).[21]

Williams encourages us, as we deal with individual emotions, to consider the context in which those emotions arise. In what ways do they emerge from the political and economic realities of a culture structured to benefit patriarchal white-body supremacy?

Williams shared his concern with me about the message people are getting if we infer that it is a law of the universe that we create our own suffering by our thinking. If we are not careful in our explanation of mindfulness, he notes, we are "weaponizing mindfulness." Often those of us who teach mindfulness help people gain awareness of internal messages that are causing them difficulty. But we do not unpack the causes of those messages. People may go away believing such thoughts are purely of their own making, rather than understanding that these messages come from society and that it is largely society that needs to change. We may be using mindfulness negatively, as a weapon, if we are not rigorous and careful in our teaching. Williams emphasizes that "those who suffer at the hands of patriarchy and racism and sexism will begin to believe all their negative emotions and feelings are their own fault—all because they must not be thinking properly."[22]

Using mindfulness techniques, Williams has developed what he calls Freedom Meditation. He differentiates between being mindful, which we can do at any moment and in any given activity, and meditation, when we sit quietly shifting our awareness to our body, mind, and emotions. Freedom Meditation includes developing an awareness that (1) noticing your own thoughts and triggers in body and mind can shift your reactivity to them; and (2) you alone are not responsible for the causes of your suffering. He asserts that by learning to shift our awareness and reactivity in this way, we will collectively change the culture of oppression.[23]

---

21. Williams, *Stay Woke*, 32–33.
22. Justin Michael Williams, interview by author, March 10, 2021.
23. Williams, *Stay Woke*, Ch. 1, "The Truth Will Set Us Free."

Are We Being Mindful about Mindfulness?

In Western culture, mindfulness has not focused on the alleviation of collective suffering, except through wishing others to be happy (as in the lovingkindness practice). It has been geared toward liberating the self, and even then, often only particular types of selves that have the privilege of isolating from community. This self-help technique has also been co-opted corporately to enable you to lessen your stress and be more productive, thus making the alleviation of stress your responsibility, even if the stressors are generated by the very entity, be it a corporation or society, bringing the mindfulness practices to you. It has indeed become over a billion-dollar industry, whose most important raw material for production is you.

Moreover, as long as the subject of liberation is myself, I do not have to have even an iota of awareness of my own privilege (if I am in a privileged category) in order to feel I am becoming liberated in mind, body, and emotion. The sole focus on the individual self may, in fact, prevent us from seeing the structural racism or sexism in our society. For example, if I am in a privileged position in this society, I can exist in a nondiverse religious or geographic community, blissfully unaware of the suffering of people who are not like me; or I can work for a company that includes racist and sexist policies and be more productive through mindfulness without any awareness of those policies if they do not personally affect me in some emotional way. If my focus is only on my own inner peace, I can go on living my life without any awareness that these realities exist and that they shape both my life and our collective lives. I really can.

Recall teacher Melvin Escobar's comment that participants in meditation have every right to be angry. The assumption that emotion is individually generated, without awareness of the historically, economically constructed misogynist and white-body culture of our Western world, may just be one more way of upholding the power of the status quo through the illusion that individuals can solve suffering on their own.

I hope it is clear by now that the criticism of mindfulness being used in purposive ways, such as to liberate the minds of a particular subset of privileged individuals, is absolutely right on. We have noted criticism by Buddhist teachers who understand mindfulness as solely about gaining present focus, not bringing about purposive ends. Their critique of the way mindfulness has been adopted into our culture from Eastern practices of meditation includes a concern that it has been co-opted as a means toward achieving particular goals.

Indeed it has, and I do not believe mindfulness can be understood in any other way than as purposive as it has been absorbed within Western culture. I mean this in a negative sense but also find potential in this realization. The corporatization of mindfulness is clearly purposive toward higher profit margins and is easily criticized. Mindfulness is also purposive in bringing people "happiness," although as we have examined, the happiness driven by the mindfulness market may, when left unexamined, be supporting the very stress-inducing societal machine mindfulness purports to combat.

But mindfulness could also be used in purposive ways we might view as positive for liberatory purposes. We catch a glimpse of this, for example, as it is interwoven with Justin's Freedom Meditation. Mindfulness tools could be incorporated for the purpose of awakening to your oppression by and/or complicity in unjust structures embedded within the society in which you live.

Once we embrace the notion that in Western culture, mindfulness *will* be used for one purpose or another, we are ready to be intentional about just what that purpose is. Mindfulness has become embedded within Western culture, where it will be used as a means to an end, which portends if we do not choose that end, we may be supporting the very culture that produces the enormous stress we offer mindfulness to help people cope with. How can we incorporate an end that promotes liberation from an oppressive culture? In Part Two, we will explore whether one answer could be coupling mindfulness with ethics and practices embedded within wisdom and faith traditions.

Part Two

Liberating Mindfulness

CHAPTER 6

Liberating Mindfulness and Religion

Mindfulness has been all about personal enhancement. How can I use mindfulness in the service of another liberation project?[1]

Several decades ago, I was invited to attend a symposium at the Garrison Institute in New York entitled "Contemplation and Community: A Symposium on the Changing Roles of University Chaplains, Spiritual Advisors and Deans of Religious Life." The event included teachings, dialogue, and experiences of silent and contemplative practices led by accomplished teachers of four spiritual traditions: Buddhism, Islam, Judaism, and Christianity.[2]

The purpose of the symposium was to inspire participants to infuse their outward work of community involvement with the wisdom gained through experiences of inner silence found in contemplation. The participants were campus-based spiritual leaders, persons "deeply committed to a wide range of social-action projects, including tutoring of disadvantaged youth, feeding the homeless, serving prison populations and providing direct assistance to impoverished

---

1. Anonymous.

2. Teachers included Father Thomas Keating, Rabbi Sheila Weinberg, Buddhist teacher Tara Brach, and Sheikh Din Muhammad Abdullah al-Dayemi.

communities in the Third World."[3] It is important to note that the spiritual leaders attending the retreat were *already* committed to social change, compassionate service, and challenging injustice. They were not learning contemplation in order to become inspired to do that work.

Following the symposium, I invited one of the teachers, Father Thomas Keating, to speak at The Common Ministry at Washington State University, where I was director at the time. He promised that if you practiced Centering Prayer (Christian silent prayer or meditation) for twenty minutes twice a day for six months, it would change your life. He was right. I happened to take my first sabbatical to write a book soon after meeting him again and took up the challenge he had given us. I gained insights into my own mind—that I would later discover mindfulness could also offer—as well as a deeper awareness of the world around me.

I also began to read works by another presenter at the Garrison Institute conference, Buddhist teacher Tara Brach, beginning with her book *Radical Acceptance*.[4] Since that time, Brach's following has increased. She currently has over 1.5 million hits on her podcasts each week and has grown to be one of the most celebrated teachers of contemporary mindfulness. She recently hosted a Radical Compassion Challenge in which she interviewed prominent figures seeking to bring about social reform in our country today.[5] She asked visionaries such as Jon Kabat-Zinn, Krista Tippett, and Elizabeth Gilbert how centering in compassion inspired each to engage in the transformative work they pursue.

As I listened to Brach's interviews, I was struck by how many of

3. Report from "Contemplation and Community: A Symposium on the Changing Roles of University Chaplains, Spiritual Advisors and Deans of Religious Life," Garrison Institute, New York, February 17–20, 2004.

4. Tara Brach, *Radical Acceptance: Embracing Your Life with the Heart of a Buddha* (New York: Bantam, 2004).

5. "Radical Compassion Challenge," April 26–May 5, 2021, https://www.tarabrach.com.

her guests were grounded not just with a commitment to compassion, but within faith traditions. I reflected on how I had recently heard Brach and other prominent mindfulness teachers refer to *spirituality* more than they had in the past.

I recall sitting with Trudy Goodman, founding teacher of InsightLA, in an empty room after participants had filed out after a Sunday morning meditation and dharma talk at the InsightLA Santa Monica. I asked to interview her because a few weeks before I thought I had heard her say, "I'm sorry, but this meditation practice *is* spirituality." After affirming that I had heard her correctly, she explained to me that spirituality, for her, is "that which is invisible to the eye, but nourishes and gives meaning to our existence—just like what happens between us as we sit here smiling at each other. But there's a lot more than what meets the eye that's also happening between us." Observing that she and I were both pleased to be with each other, learning and discovering, she said, "I call that spiritual because it matters."[6]

Brach's guests spoke not only about spirituality but about religious faith. American author and humanitarian Maria Shriver told Brach, "I was raised in a world where it was expected that you're going to be out in the world helping, you're going to be out in the world doing . . . both of my parents really saw their Catholicism as a social justice movement . . . I was raised in that culture."[7] Later in life, she discovered it might be possible to turn this compassion she had been expressing to others inwardly toward herself as well. Shriver finds that the tools of meditation, reading, walking, and writing help her to balance all her responsibilities and better pace herself. She dedicates much of her service to women and calls upon the notion of the Divine feminine and feminine warrior to help her make sense of all she is experiencing. Shriver credits her Catholic upbringing for teaching

---

6. Trudy Goodman, interview by author, Santa Monica, CA, July 28, 2019.

7. "Radical Compassion Challenge."

her about service, such as when she worked in food kitchens to serve people who were food insecure, as a regular part of growing up in the Kennedy family.

Valarie Kaur, lawyer and Sikh activist, also draws on the woman-warrior image. She discussed with Brach her call for "revolutionary love." For Kaur, loving others, even your opponents, stems from the core teachings of Sikhism, including the Sikh warrior tradition. This tradition presents nonviolent action as "fierce, strategic, demanding, and disciplined."[8] Her contemplation and activism are born from her grandfather's stories from within the Sikh faith, and now she is raising her own son and daughter with these stories.

Van Jones, news commentator and politically involved change-maker, was also a featured guest interviewed by Brach. Jones, who is engaged in revolutionary work on issues of poverty and incarceration, describes himself as a person of faith. He regrets that liberal Americans at times scoff at those, like him, who champion liberal causes yet also consider themselves to be religious. These critics seem to ignore the powerful motivation for justice that faith can provide and reduce religiosity to uncritical adoption of an untenable belief system. He notes the irony that conservative Americans do not consider the study of sacred texts or embracing spirituality as obstacles to critical thinking or as signs of a lack of intelligence. Jones writes, "As some liberal activists get more spiritual, and many spiritual people join more social-change causes, I see real hope at the crossroads."[9]

I began to wonder; what if a person's faith or underlying philosophical or ethical tradition is not just something they reference now and then, but might actually be *necessary* as a foundation for how one uses mindfulness or engages in meditation? In other words, what if

---

8. Valarie Kaur, *See No Stranger: A Memoir and Manifesto of Revolutionary Love* (New York: One World, 2020), 97.

9. Van Jones, *Beyond the Messy Truth* (New York: Ballantine Books, 2017), 32; see also 74, Kindle.

faith or ethical commitment itself provides the motivation for how mindfulness is used and directed?

Compulsory Secularization for Mindfulness

In Part One, we identified some largely unspoken assumptions that have grown up around mindfulness: (1) that every individual everywhere is universally under stress, and that this stress is inevitable and increasing; (2) that mindfulness is currently claimed to be the best, if not one of the best, antidotes to alleviate that stress, shift your relationship to your personal emotions, and bring true happiness to you and every individual who practices it; and (3) that the happiness individuals have gained through mindfulness will automatically rub off and bring happiness to society. Let me add a fourth assumption widely accepted in our country regarding mindfulness: that it must be secularized.

In every mindfulness course I have taken, the assumption has been clear (whether explicitly stated or not) that mindfulness must be secularized and separated from any communal religious context in order to be seen as valid and universally accessible. This comes with one caveat: there is general agreement that practitioners and teachers of mindfulness can be philosophically Buddhist and practicing a particular Westernized style of Buddhism. Even then, mindfulness must be taught in a way that is accessible to everyone (even though in practice it is often particularly geared toward those who identify as either "spiritual but not religious" or Buddhist). In popular culture, it is seen as an individual pursuit, separated from any specific religious or spiritual tradition.

The effort to take the truths of Buddhism, secularize them, evangelize them to a culture very different from that of their origin, and then insist they are universally applicable sounds a lot like cultural appropriation or even colonization. What we fail to notice is how mindfulness has taken on dominant, Western, white cultural values; how it is embedded within a cultural celebration of individualism;

how it is intertwined with practices of unquestioned consumption; and how it has been transformed into an essential object of happiness today, as we noted in chapter 3.

Can mindfulness tools, rather than being co-opted for unquestioned cultural purposes, instead be utilized in ways that challenge cultural oppressions based on race, class, or gender? I began to discover spaces where meditation and contemplative practices have been offering just such a challenge to culture for a long time. As I embarked on an investigation of mindfulness alongside my own spiritual journey, one of the great mysteries that emerged was the intentionality, or we might say purposiveness, that emerges from faith—faith that the world can be a place where an ethic of pursuing justice is central.

Liberating Religion with Mindfulness

Jim Burklo observes that the subject of mindfulness most often begins with the self, with the individual who is practicing mindfulness. But when you move into the realm of the sacred, the subject is not the self; rather, it is what he calls "Awe."[10] It is Awe of a creator, which many traditions will discover includes the self, for Awe is found within oneself as well as encompassing all of life. Great interest has been developing in the concept of Awe and its effect on individuals, whether secular, spiritual, or religious. Persons who report having experiences of Awe are found to have a greater sense of their interconnectedness with others—even outside of their own social categories—a stronger sense of humility, and a diminished sense of ego, than persons reporting experiences of joy or amusement. Researchers have called the experience of Awe an emotion with moral, aesthetic, and spiritual dimensions.[11] Recently, researchers have found that Awe correlates

---

10. Jim Burklo, *Mindful Christianity* (Haworth, NJ: St. Johann Press, 2017), 14–16.

11. Dacher Keltner and Jonathan Haidt, "Approaching Awe, a Moral, Spiritual and Aesthetic Emotion," *Cognition and Emotion* 17, no. 2 (2003): 297–314.

with an immediate reduction in a person's level of daily stress.[12] Like scientific studies showing that long-term meditation and contemplative practices shift the way our brains work, this is another example of where research is corroborating what persons of faith have experienced for centuries.

If mindfulness has liberated us from religion, perhaps it is time that we liberate religion with mindfulness.[13] If we allow mindfulness tools to be taught within a cultural base of a spiritual or religious context, we might discover Awe—or, as we might simply say in mindfulness terms, Presence—in a fresh way. Along my journey, in fact, I discovered that mindfulness was present deep within faith traditions, often hidden from us by the tradition's outer trappings. And I began to suspect that the accessibility of classical mindfulness tools might be a key with which to explore the aspects of mindfulness contained within those traditions.

Teachers utilizing mindfulness tools for liberatory purposes alongside the spiritual practices of one's roots, particularly with the goal of addressing societal injustice, are on the rise. We see this particularly in those working for healing from systematic racism. Resmaa Menakem highlights body-centered methods, including "Individual and collective humming, rocking, rhythmic clapping, drumming, singing, grounding touch, wailing circles, and call and response, to name just a few."[14] These are found within African spirituality that dates back generations. The settling of the body is the beginning of healing, but according to Menakem, it only works when one recognizes the various contexts in which a body and its ancestry are shaped

---

12. Yang Bai et al., "Awe, Daily Stress, and Elevated Life Satisfaction," *Journal of Personality and Social Psychology* 120, no. 4 (April 2021): 837–60.

13. Burklo, *Mindful Christianity*, 2.

14. Resmaa Menakem, *My Grandmother's Hands: Racialized Trauma and the Pathway to Mending Our Hearts and Bodies* (Las Vegas, NV: Central Recovery Press, 2017), 15, Kindle. See also chapter 10, "Your Soul Nerve," for explanations and instructions on the practices.

and lived. Not recognizing this amounts to avoidance of healing. Mindfully incorporated, these practices enable persons to access in a somatic way the deep, persistent trauma carried within their bodies. They are methodologies, as Terrence put it in chapter 5, that call on communal spiritual African roots of Black humanity. Terrence seeks to unlock practices today toward this end, even as he is engaging in a traditional mindfulness teacher-training program.

Justin Michael Williams incorporates visualizations into his Freedom Meditation. These include drawing on deep faith and compassion by visualizing ancestors, known and unknown. He encourages meditators to call on those who are especially nurturing, like his own grandmother, whom he calls Baca, and bring forth awareness of those against whom you are prejudiced. He encourages bringing to light all of your societally induced self-sabotage or sabotage against others, and all of your racist or homophobic attitudes or other complicity. He writes, "This is our time to wake up, my brothers and sisters. This is our time to rise. And we rise together."[15]

Justice Crudup brings the mindfulness and equanimity he learned in his Buddhist practice to his work helping young people affectively speak, protest, and enact legislative change for racial justice. Throughout the year in which Black Lives Matter got enormous traction, in the middle of the COVID-19 pandemic, Justice says he truly came to understand and celebrate what it means to be a Black man. While he was working a day job at a law firm, he began forming a nonprofit organization to help young people discover their power and their voice, and to help them to see that after the protest comes the hard work of legislation, if we are to move toward societal justice. Justice shared with me:

> Last year was a turning point in my life in that I really took the time to learn about my Blackness, and what it means to be Black, and how beautiful it is and how strong it is. Which really

---

15. Justin Michael Williams, *Stay Woke* (Louisville, CO: Sounds True Publishing. 2020), 278. Kindle.

empowered me—it was very emotional for me. In a sense, it really empowered me to talk to other individuals who are Black in Orange County and figure out their experience and see how we can all come together.[16]

Justice created a nonprofit organization to help young people learn to agitate through protest but also to translate their agitation further into legislative changes. Throughout 2020, he was part of many movements and organized and led some fifty protests throughout Orange County. "I was called to lead so many individuals that were suffering. Just to let them grieve and to empower themselves and to be motivated, which then turned into me creating a nonprofit organization."[17]

I met with Justice when he was invited to Chapman University to help organize a protest with our Asian American Pacific Islander (AAPI) students. As I listened to the students speak of their experiences of being ignored, hated, and silenced, I thanked him for giving them the opportunity to share in this way. Yes, he acknowledged, they really needed to grieve.

For Justice, meditation has offered a way of life. Rather than something you just have to sit down and practice every day, once you accept the disciplines, the precepts, and join with a community or sangha, mindfulness and a sense of equanimity begin to make sense to you and to come naturally. Justice is engaged in compassionate agitation, helping these young people bring awareness to the conditions and emotions of their lives.

Many more teachers are connecting classical mindfulness tools with traditional chanting, music, communal ritual, and activism. This is a movement utilizing Mindfulness for Liberation, which is the title Shelly Harrell uses for bringing mindfulness tools into the practice of developing awareness of race-related experiences.[18] Her incorporation of meditative practices such as chanting and listening

---

16. Justice Crudup, interview by author, March 25, 2021.

17. Justice Crudup, interview.

18. Dr. Shelly P. Harrell, https://www.drshellyharrell.com.

to the music of Ray Charles allows people to take the courageous step of increasing their awareness of what arises when they consider their experiences of race and racism.

By combining mindfulness meditation tools with ancestral and spiritual roots, these teachers and practitioners are uncovering the deep connections between personal well-being and the sociopolitical contexts of persons and communities.

The Practices of RAIN and RAINN

I learned a mindfulness practice called RAIN many years ago, a version of which has been popularized by teacher and author Tara Brach. The original meditation was introduced by teacher Michele McDonald,[19] and the acronym stood for: *recognize, allow, investigate, non-identify* (or *non-attach*). You begin by recognizing what presents itself (an emotion, thought, sensation, etc.) and seeing if you can simply allow it to be present. You then investigate. I tell people I work with that this step of RAIN is not the kind of investigation that occurs when you tell a problem to a psychoanalyst, to which the psychoanalyst replies, "Tell me about your mother." It's not that kind of digging into the psyche—which can also be useful and necessary! Rather, you show some interest in what comes up, getting curious about it. Finally, you let go of its hold on you. This is the step of non-identifying or non-attaching. It does not mean a once-and-for-all ridding of your identity (a criticism raised by BIPOC folks for whom identity is sometimes all one might have to cling to) but rather gaining distance from troubling, haunting thoughts and emotions.

I first learned this practice from The Power of Awareness, an online course I took quite a few years ago, taught by mindfulness teachers Tara Brach and Jack Kornfield. For many, many months after taking the course I returned to the recording of the guided RAIN meditation. Whenever I felt uncertainty about why I was feeling off-kilter

---

19. Tara Brach, *Radical Compassion: Learning to Love Yourself and Your World with the Practice of RAIN* (New York: Viking, 2019), xx.

or exactly what emotions were occurring, this particular meditation would offer me great clarity.

When I returned to the recording recently, I discovered that the meditation had been altered and the online guided meditation from that former course changed. I realized that the change likely reflected Brach's shift toward adding an aspect of *refuge* into the mindfulness practice of RAIN, as outlined in her book *Radical Compassion*. Instead of *non-attach*, the final movement of the meditation is now *nurture*. Following internal investigation, Brach encourages you to draw on inner resources for self-nurture. These might include beings important in your life whose strength you might be able to draw on, such as a spiritual figure or a parent. "After the RAIN," once the meditation is over, she suggests you might allow yourself to shift from "doing to being," possibly experiencing a quality of more open presence.[20]

I initially struggled to understand why I was so disappointed with the shift in terminology from *non-attachment* to *nurture* when I returned to follow the instructions for RAIN in The Power of Awareness course. I now realize that it was because the earlier usage of *non-attachment* allowed me to work with myself and students to discover where a difficult, persistent thought or emotion may have originated. Many of our emotions arise in reaction to spaces that we inhabit within the social order, or within racial structures of our society, or within a gendered hierarchy. That recognition can move us to understand we can heal, as well as that the structures of society need to be transformed.

In sharing mindfulness, I introduce a process I call RAINN. It is based on many aspects of RAIN but includes nurture as well as non-attachment with regard to culturally induced thoughts or emotions. As we have discussed, sometimes even mindfulness is used in a way that asks you to toe the party line, to be compliant and self-focused. The following RAINN practice helps to widen your awareness of

---

20. Brach, *Radical Compassion*, 45.

yourself, and beyond yourself. You may find it is useful if you are in the midst of a difficult situation or feeling stuck.

RAINN Practice

This is a practice you can try on your own, or with a trusted friend or group. Because it can stir unexpected emotions—you might have in mind someone you can talk with, or a journal to write in afterward.

Sit comfortably, close your eyes, and rest your attention internally.

Recognize what is occurring right now. What thought is here? Do you feel a specific emotion? Do you feel tension in your body?

Allow: Ask yourself if you are able to allow this thought, emotion, or sensation to be here right now. Can you let it be? If this feels intense, you might give it even 30 percent of your attention, with the rest on your breath or resting in your body.

Interest: Show some gentle interest to investigate what is here. Is the thought connected to any specific emotion? Can you label the emotion? Sometimes landing on the right label offers a subtle release inside. Ask: What am I believing about myself right now? Am I supposed to be perfect, or am I unworthy, for example?

Nurture: Ask, what does this vulnerable part of me need right now? Can I call upon God, or a higher self, or a person who loves me unconditionally? Can I offer myself nurture?

Non-Attach: Slowly let go and identify less with this thought and emotion, allowing them to fade as though you are setting them on a cloud and watching them drift away. Let yourself simply be. Remind yourself: I am not this thought; I am not this emotion. They are simply guests (however unwanted) here right now. Ask yourself: are these messages I believe about myself mine alone?

Move from doing to being as you let go. Eventually, you may gradually move back to doing as you join with a community toward dismantling unhealthy societal causes of these messages.

RAINN: Clairre's Backstory

Several years before her wedding, Clairre came to see me in my office after being referred to me by another professor.[21] She was highly agitated and troubled, asking questions about her faith and a blossoming relationship. She had recently met a young man she felt deeply compatible with, and he seemed equally interested in her. They met in person, but he then returned to his native Scotland, and they were now carrying on a long-distance relationship between Scotland and California.

One day, she appeared particularly upset. She had learned more about her boyfriend's ex-girlfriend, whom Clairre described as blond, thin, and beautiful—the ideal (according to Clairre) of both Scottish and American beauty. Clairre is of Persian descent, with olive skin and thick, wavy, black hair. Clairre was absolutely convinced that he was still more attracted to his ex-girlfriend than to her, and she could not let go of her deep fear and anxiety.

We discussed what his actions showed. By all accounts, he was attentive and clearly interested in a relationship with Clairre. So were her fears justified? I asked her whether she had any evidence he was still obsessed with his ex-girlfriend. Maybe not, she said, but her fears were still overwhelming her.

We went through an exercise in which I walked her through the first four movements of RAINN—with Clairre first settling in her body, then recognizing and allowing her thoughts to be present, and then noting, even naming her emotions. She investigated the connection between her thoughts, her anxiety and fear, and experienced the way it manifested in tension in her body. She was able to bring nurture to herself, drawing on the love of her father and her faith.

When we finished, Clairre felt more grounded. She said she knew what she was feeling was irrational, but she couldn't shake it. I asked her if she was willing to continue just a bit more. Could she non-attach just enough from her feelings of unworthiness to ask whether

---

21. I first introduced Clairre in chapter 4.

she had any idea where these ideas might have come from—such as why would she think her current boyfriend's ex-girlfriend was more attractive to him?

Of course, she realized, it is because of the air we breathe: every commercial, every film, every message she received growing up told her that anyone with darker skin and hair was less attractive. Our society also sends the message that a woman must compete for a man by being more physically attractive, according to societal standards, than other women he might encounter. The competition between women for men's attention is culturally ingrained in young girls. It was not until this awareness arose that she was able to gradually let go of her fear and to trust what was true—that he showed Clairre his undivided attention.

Clairre bit the bullet and took an internship in the United Kingdom, where she had the opportunity to visit the small village her boyfriend lived in and to meet his family. We continued to correspond and to meet when she returned to California. Her concerns now often centered around possible conflicts between his agnosticism and her Christian faith. In time, she experienced how the love they shared could allow them to respect each other, even though they might disagree on religion. And as you saw in chapter 4, they eventually got married and have a strong relationship today.

As we continue with Part Two, we'll look at the ways faith offers a deep basis for mindful, compassionate transformation of self and society. We'll discover that meditative practices are present in many faith traditions and consider whether mindfulness tools might help to bring these to better focus. As an interfaith teacher and dean, I have learned to step carefully and not conflate one religion with another. I will be cautious here as well, attempting to keep intact the integrity of each tradition.

There is shared experience among religions, however, such as in a sense of Awe. With thoughtfulness and clarity, mindfulness tools might be combined with other ancient practices that are already embedded with theological and ethical urges toward communal liberation.

Throughout my spiritual journey and professional career, I have been invited into sacred meditative and communal spaces held by various religions, which I will explore in chapter 8. I delve most deeply, however, in chapters 9 and 10 into the one I am most familiar with: Christianity. But first, we turn to the tradition most associated with the mindfulness movement today. What can we learn from Buddhism?

CHAPTER 7

What Can We Learn from Buddhism?

Are we willing to see that sometimes mindfulness can make us less functional in the world, that it makes us less willing to betray our morals, less willing to betray the carefulness of our heart?[1]

Sipping tea in my new friend's favorite coffee shop a few blocks from the University of Edinburgh, I glanced at my watch, realizing I had completely lost track of time. I did not mean to keep you too long, I said to my friend, and he replied that he did have an appointment at 11:00 this morning (it was now well past 11:00), but he thought they could go on without him. We continued talking for another full hour. I was struck by his compassionate nature as we spoke.

Avinash Bansode worked as a doctor and general practitioner for many years after first encountering meditation in his native India. Now, married and the father of a six-year-old son, he has developed a career integrating mindfulness and medicine. Founder and director of Mindfullybeing, he pioneered the Mindfulness Initiative through the Chaplaincy Center at the University of Edinburgh, receiving an Impact Award in 2017 for his unique approach.

I asked him what he sees as the heart of mindfulness right now. He described it as "the heart coming back to the heart." He admits this is

---

1. Jesse Maceo Vega-Frey, dhamma talk, Vipassana Hawaii Retreat, November 27–December 2, 2020.

96

a complex message to get across, though, in the current buzzy sound-bites of mindfulness in the media. Ideally, Avinash's practice involves holding the heart flame of awareness that, at its core, is ethical and filled with compassion. "Mindful Awareness" is subtle energy, he tells me, and it is crucial to align it with what is good and skillful rather than what is unskillful and harmful. He suggests that we have to go back to the source for this alignment, to the heart of mindful awareness traditions, especially early Indian Buddhist philosophy.[2]

Yet, how do those who practice Buddhism, especially those in the East who are steeped in its early roots, view contemporary mindfulness? Avinash admits, "My Buddhist friends are doubtful about the secular mindful movement and think I'm not a proper Buddhist because I teach mindfulness without the Buddha-dharma." To which he replies, "Just because Newton discovered gravity, gravity is not Newtonian; likewise, Buddha's formula for mindfulness doesn't make mindfulness a Buddhist phenomenon." Just as gravity is natural and attracts everything, he sees mindful awareness as a fundamental practice, capable of naturally holding and balancing us.[3]

Alternatively, some who adopt Buddhist ideas, especially those studying contemporary Western mindfulness, can conflate Buddhism and mindfulness as though they are one and the same. Recall the experience of Terrence in the mindfulness teacher-training course, where some were concerned about separating themselves from religious community and history as they equated mindfulness with Buddhism, and Buddhism with religion.

I had just finished writing a draft of this chapter when I received an email from a former student, Sophia Barr, asking if we could talk about this very idea. She was practicing mindfulness, having learned classical mindfulness in a course with me and subsequently taking several intense courses on Eastern traditions, including Buddhism.

---

2. Avinash Bansode, interview by author, Edinburgh, Scotland, September 25, 2019.

3. Avinash Bansode, email correspondence with author, July 22, 2021.

Confused about some issues she was dealing with in her life in light of this learning, she wanted to ask about them. She was wondering whether it goes against mindfulness and Buddhist principles to try to change some of the conditions and circumstances in her life. When we met soon after, she explained her confusion:

> Let's say there is a relationship or there's a situation and it's not ideal. It's not what you were expecting or it's not what you want. And the Buddhist ideal tells you to accept life as it is, and see what you have, and that you have everything that you need. Well, what about making changes, and when can you make those changes?[4]

I asked Sophia whether she considers herself a Buddhist or if there is a religion or philosophy or particular set of values she aligns herself with. She said she meditates and practices mindfulness but is not part of an organized group. She thought about where her values come from. "I think a lot of them come from Buddhism lately in my studies, because I really believe in the ideas—they include things I really align with." She listed the oneness of all people, the goodness of all people, the importance of listening, removing the ego, developing nonreactivity, and being present while not forgetting the past.

Sophia is one of the most serious and thoughtful students I have encountered. She truly desires to live a mindful and meaningful life. And we see her confusion as she practices mindfulness, begins to learn about Eastern religions, and attempts to apply their values and insights within her own Western context as a young American university student.

It can be very confusing to try to take the meditative, mindful message of Buddhism, which directs a person to be nonjudgmental about what is good or bad, and set it into a culture in which systematic injustices such as misogyny and racism are deeply imbedded. As we saw above, for example, Sophia's attempt to do so leaves her won-

---

4. Sophia Barr, conversation with author, January 20, 2021.

dering whether a person should just accept staying in a relationship that may be toxic.

Mindfulness and Buddhism have often been conflated within the American psyche, and so they are deeply interconnected in the minds of many practitioners. But is Buddhism simply mindfulness? If not— if it is more than mindfulness or if it is distinct from mindfulness— what can we as mindfulness practitioners learn from Buddhism? And is it possible for any of us to completely intertwine the projects of social liberation and liberation of the mind?

The Four Noble Truths

When I learned the Four Noble Truths of Buddhism, I felt as though I had discovered the truth of the human experience. And when I read Jack Kornfield's book on what he calls "universal teachings" drawn from Buddhism, I devoured it.[5] For a feminist who is wary of universals collapsing women or any group into universal categories, this is something! There are many ways to practice Buddhism, yet the Four Noble Truths are a foundational teaching of the Buddha.

What does it mean to say something is true? "Is it really true?" we'll ask, after hearing about a surprising occurrence. "The truth is," we'll say. "True story" can mean a story is literally true, but there can also be truth in a story in the sense that there is an underlying moral within it, even if the actual events never took place. Politically, especially in recent years, possession of the truth is claimed by diametrically opposing sides; it seems no longer to be dependent on facts but has instead come to represent a preferred point of view.

Truth need not be the same as universality, which implies that in every instance, in every context, something is applicable and useful as a descriptor, a practice, and a predictor. In *Why Buddhism Is True*, Robert Wright admits that we have to be suspicious about the word *truth*, yet he says that he generally finds Buddhist philosophy

---

5. Jack Kornfield, *The Wise Heart: A Guide to the Universal Teachings of Buddhist Psychology* (New York: Bantam, 2008).

to realistically describe reality. He posits that if you set out to rid yourself of suffering by accepting the Four Noble Truths, you would generally also have a clearer understanding of reality, apart from what may simply be your perception of reality.[6] Buddhists call our warped perception of the truth of reality *delusion*.

The first of the Four Noble Truths states that there is suffering, that, by its very nature, human existence includes suffering. The Second Noble Truth says that suffering has a cause, which is human attachment or desire. The Third Noble Truth states that there is a way out of this suffering or dissatisfaction. Finally, the Fourth Noble Truth offers a way out, through practicing the Noble Eightfold Path of Buddhism.

That there is suffering seems a given, in my experience, and I suspect in yours as well. That the suffering is caused by attachment or desire makes sense as well. Just imagine, if we were not attached to something, like a relationship, the way our body looks or moves, specific foods, our car or home, or our dreams for the future, we would not suffer when any of those were taken away, changed, or simply ended.

That there is a way out of this suffering brings great hope; and the actual way out itself is where I have realized that Buddhism is not just a philosophy, it is a practice, one that involves mental discipline, a commitment to ethical conduct, and the development of wisdom. The path out of suffering entails discipline in every aspect of your life.

The eight elements of the Eightfold Path can be imagined in three categories that make up the legs on a three-legged stool; each is needed to maintain the stability of the stool. The first leg focuses on moral conduct and ethics in one's life and actions: *Right Speech, Right Action,* and *Right Livelihood.* These indicate that what you say, what you do, and how you make a living should always be life-

6. Robert Wright, *Why Buddhism Is True* (New York: Simon & Schuster, 2017), 263.

giving, acknowledging that your speech and action deeply affect others.

A second leg on the Eightfold Path provides a foundation for meditation in which one hones the states of mind needed to develop wisdom. *Right Effort* includes ridding oneself of greed and ignorance and cultivating such states as equanimity and kindness. *Right Mindfulness* refers to practicing awareness of the reality of how all things come and go or arise and fade. *Right Concentration* involves developing clear and careful focus in all a person does.

The third leg on the Eightfold Path includes two final practices toward the development of wisdom. *Right Understanding* (or *View*) and *Right Thought* (or *Intent* or *Resolve*) refer to seeing and thinking about reality with enough detachment not to take everything personally, and to be more centered on deeper understanding and love.

So, we see that the development of mindfulness is woven into the steps of Buddhism's Eightfold Path. But it is important to note that mindfulness is just one practice toward liberation of thought and mind, an observation many Buddhist practitioners have pointed out.[7] Various Buddhist practices are complex and multiple.

Mindfulness Arises from Buddhism

Several strains of Buddhism have been readily integrated into Western society over the past decades. For example, one teacher who has contributed to the prevalence of present-day mindfulness in the West is Vietnamese monk Thich Nhat Hanh. As taught by Thich Nhat Hahn, mindfulness emerges from Vietnamese Buddhist practice within the Mahayana tradition, one of the major forms of Buddhism. Western mindfulness enthusiasts rush to read his bestselling book

---

7. Lynette M. Monteiro, R. F. Musten, and Jane Compson, "Traditional and Contemporary Mindfulness: Finding the Middle Path in the Tangle of Concerns," *Mindfulness* 6, no. 1 (2015): 1–13; and Christopher Titmuss, "The Buddha of Mindfulness: A Stress Destruction Programme," July 13, 2013, https://www.christophertitmussblog.org.

The Miracle of Mindfulness, which describes how to live a fuller life, seeking a consciousness that is alive to the present moment.[8] Yet he and his small group of monks exercised great care, discipline, and dedication to social concern and peace over many years to develop their commitment to meditation in the midst of their work of service.[9]

For our purposes, I will focus on the impact of the teachings of Mahasi Sayadaw, a Burmese monk who has been influential on the teachers from whom I have learned vipassana (insight meditation), a type of Buddhist meditation practice. He draws from the Theravadan form, another major Buddhist tradition, as it was developed in Burma. Mahasi Sayadaw set out to make the path to enlightenment available to everyone—East and West, monk and layperson. A number of Americans who are now prominent mindfulness teachers studied this tradition with him or with his disciples.[10]

Vipassana offers practices for developing a relationship with everything that is occurring and then letting go of that relationship as a new opportunity appears. Mahasi Sayadaw described a central practice of "bare attention" in meditation to achieve liberation of heart and mind. It can be described as having a soft readiness for whatever conditions you may find yourself in. As his student Sayadaw U Pandita simply says, "Objects of the past are no more. Objects of the future have not arisen yet."[11]

Mahasi Sayadaw's methods have been criticized for minimizing and essentializing Buddhism to an acultural practice, one that is able

8. Thich Nhat Hanh, *The Miracle of Mindfulness: An Introduction to the Practice of Meditation* (trans. Mobi Ho; Boston: Beacon Press, 1975), 11.

9. Thich Nhat Hanh, *Interbeing* (ed. Fred Eppsteiner; Berkeley, CA: Parallax Press, 1993), editor's introduction.

10. See Jeff Wilson, *Mindful America: The Mutual Transformation of Buddhist Meditation and American Culture* (New York: Oxford University Press, 2014), for a detailed history of the emergence of mindfulness in the West.

11. Sayadaw U. Pandita, *The State of Mind Called Beautiful* (ed. Kate Wheeler; trans. Venerable Vivekānanda; Somerville, MA: Wisdom Publications, 2006), 96–97.

to bring full consciousness and fullness of life to any practitioner, regardless of their faith tradition. One objection is to his focus on mindful meditation without requiring either skilled concentration or familiarity with Buddhist philosophy and its traditional renunciations. Enlightenment, it is argued, seems to be attainable in remarkably short amounts of time, and ethical judgment is not emphasized strongly enough.[12]

Yet, while Sayadaw is criticized for developing a system of meditation practice to offer laypersons a path to liberation, his writings are filled with insistence on the difficulty of practice that is embedded within a moral context. And his student, Sayadaw U Pandita, does focus on ethical observances and conduct, offering the teachings of the Buddha to laypeople so that they may be freed from suffering and help others be free. The teachings, which can result in "liberating insight," are drawn from the code of conduct for monks, which he reduces to five basic ethical observances for laypeople.[13] But although he simplifies the code of conduct, it does not disappear, and remains primary in his teachings. In his book *In This Very Life*, he outlines the teachings of the Buddha and begins with basic morality and meditation instructions.[14] His teachings are also filled with the development of *metta* meditation imbued with kindness and love. This kindness is incorporated in simple meditations on the care with which you observe how everything comes and goes, even observing one breath or one sound at a time. Here is an example of insight meditation you might try:[15]

---

12. Robert H. Scharf, "Epilogue: Is Mindfulness Buddhist? [And Why It Matters]," in Robert Meikyo Rosenbaum and Barry Magid, eds., *What's Wrong with Mindfulness (and What Isn't): Zen Perspectives* (Somerville, MA: Wisdom Publications, 2016), 145.

13. See U Pandita, *The State of Mind Called Beautiful*.

14. Sayadaw U Pandita, *In This Very Life* (ed. Kate Wheeler; trans. Venerable Vivekānanda; Somerville, MA: Wisdom Publications, 1992), 1–3.

15. See U Pandita, *In This Very Life*, 4–6, for extended instructions.

An Insight Meditation

- Imagine your task is simply to accompany what is occurring and to observe the nature of the way things are, aware of the reality of life as all things come and go.
- Sit upright and close your eyes. Bring your attention to your abdomen and breathe normally. Allow yourself to notice sensations of rising and falling, and sharpen your attention to observe an entire breath, then another. You might add a soft mental note of *rising, falling*.
- When you find yourself distracted with a thought, note this with a silent label: *thinking, thinking*. Become aware of any direct experience of a physical sensation, such as a sound, smell, and so on, similarly labeling them (*hearing, hearing*), then return to observe the rising and falling of your breath.

Mindfulness in Vipassana Practice

As I read the works of Sayadaw and his successors, without dismissing the objections of Buddhist critics, it is clear that the attention he instructs you to pay in meditation is far from what contemporary mindfulness encourages. His teachings emphasize the cultivation of morality in every aspect of your life. In contrast, as we have seen, mindfulness is thought of by millions in the West today as a way of helping you to cope so you can be better at your job, a better investor, or a better lover. It is thought that everything will go more smoothly in your life because you are more mindful. But as Jesse Maceo Vega-Frey, a teacher within Sayadaw's lineage, argues, "Mindfulness isn't designed for that. Mindfulness isn't designed to make samsara work better and to get you to win at this game, because the game can't be won."[16]

---

16. Vega-Frey, dhamma talk.

Samsara refers to the cycle humans are caught in—a cycle of life, death, and rebirth we are trapped in due to ignorance, aversion, and craving. Liberation from this tyranny of the heart and mind has nothing to do with success in today's consumerist environment. In vipassana practice, the unwillingness to betray your own heart is what it means to take care of yourself. The practice, Jesse asserts, may actually put us on the fringe of society, rather than happily benefitting from our place within it. Describing the difference between vipassana meditation and contemporary mindfulness, he writes, "Instead of complete liberation from greed, hatred, and delusion, the utter destruction of suffering, and final relief from madness of craving, people are perversely ambitious to be '10% happier.'"[17]

I spoke with Jesse and his teacher, Michele McDonald, at the charming and rustic Pomaikai Café in Kapa'au on the Big Island of Hawaii. We arrived just as the café was closing and found we had the place to ourselves. We sat around a large wooden picnic table out back, surrounded by lush green foliage under the shade of a covered patio, talking about mindfulness and Buddhism. Then we drove to the true northernmost tip of the island to hike through ancient, sacred forest and stand upon a cliff overlooking the breathtaking coastline.

Michele remarked on how complex the introduction of Buddhism to Western culture has been. McDonald, the first woman to teach a formal retreat in Burma within this lineage, cofounded Vipassana Hawaii with Steven Smith. She suggests that some of the evolution of Buddhism into the West has been healing, like the openness to the feminine and to women as leaders and practitioners. But our culture has also changed Buddhism and mindfulness into a commodity. Compulsory secularization has made it possible for that to happen, Michele shares. She finds it sad when someone is "afraid to empha-

---

17. Jesse Maceo Vega-Frey, *Insurgent Heart: A Vipassana Manual for the Guerrilla Yogi* (Mountain View, CA: Do Less for Peace, 2020), loc. 386, Kindle.

size ethics because people won't like it." As a result, mindfulness has become whatever the presenter of mindfulness thinks people want to hear.[18]

Lest one believe that vipassana Buddhist practice is easy, one need only read Vega-Frey's book *Insurgent Heart: A Vipassana Manual for the Guerrilla Yogi.* In it, you will encounter the unexpected and gain a much deeper understanding of what practicing vipassana is about, including its revolutionary character. Jesse compares his lineage's approach to vipassana with guerilla warfare, citing guerilla warriors and leaders—from a manual of the Irish Republican Army to teachings of Mao Tse-Tung (Zedong) to writings of Ernesto "Che" Guevara. He elicits from their tactics a foundation for the path toward enlightenment. Guerilla warfare is grueling, he writes, and at times you lose comrades or have momentary defeats and strategic retreats; but it always leads to steady progress to break down the enemy. That enemy is characterized as "Mara," the "deified personification of delusion" pulling you away from liberation. The Buddha explained his process of awakening as a battle between the armies of Mara and himself.[19] Buddhists refer to three enemies, or internal causes of suffering: greed, hatred, and the delusion that our grasping at attachments will bring satisfaction.

Tactics for battle include those perfected by disciplined guerilla fighters who are defending the people against, or overthrowing an invader with, armies hundreds of times more powerful than they are. Guerillas must know every inch of territory in order to move through it undetected. Similarly, through vipassana you learn every inch of your inner territory—your senses, emotions, thoughts, and mindstate—but your enemy, who is much stronger, only knows and travels one main road. That enemy is the inner habitual tendency toward greed, hatred, and delusion. You must intimately read the subtleties

---

18. Jesse Maceo Vega-Frey and Michele McDonald, interview by author, Kapa'au, HI, July 10, 2019.

19. Vega-Frey, *Insurgent Heart*, loc. 256 of 5695.

of nature or nearby civilizations like a native to the land in order
to know where you will find refuge from distraction and reactivity.
Other guerrilla tactics relevant to vipassana include a strategic flexi-
bility of method, the ability to retreat from intense engagement without viewing the retreat as a loss, and a fluidity within the complex
dynamics of solitude and community.

This is battle. And as in guerrilla warfare, it is a battle during
which a person may end up doing more running away than attacking.
Yet insight meditation as described through the metaphor of guerilla
warfare does not shy away from the violence done by greed, hatred,
and delusion, and the radical means to conquering those. Vipassana
practice is deeply grounded in ethical behavior and action. This takes
the form of positive moral actions rooted in generosity and kindness
as well as restraint from behaviors rooted in greed, hatred, and delusion. Jesse compares this ethical restraint to the tactics of sabotage
for the guerrilla warrior—destroying the infrastructure by which
immoral impulses lead to harmful actions in the world. What occurs
is recognition that the dynamics of oppression also operate within
oneself, just as they appear in the external environment of the guerilla warrior. Vipassana offers freedom from inner oppressive regimes,
such as the tyranny of a narcissistic ego. It encourages internal development of compassion for the self as a battleground, and the development of love, even for your enemies. It is grounded in support of your
own pathway and that of persons struggling around you. It is centered
in loyalty to the cause and the ability to shift and be flexible at any
moment just as guerilla fighters must, letting go of any one habit if it
proves to be detrimental to the overall goal of freedom.

Vipassana practice is also deeply grounded in love. There is a ten-
derheartedness, at times almost a broken-heartedness, as you observe
the cruelty of your own mind in craving and demanding so much
and offering such sharp criticism of yourself or others. As a kind of
counterbalance and a way to provide a more secure inner foundation,
vipassana is often accompanied by practice of the four *brahmaviharas*
stemming from teachings of the Buddha: *metta, karuna, mudita,*

and *uppekha*. In English they are often translated *lovingkindness, compassion, appreciative joy,* and *equanimity.* As they are cultivated, they allow and enable awareness of the depths of grief, joy, sadness, or openheartedness. They are not practiced in order to gloss over any difficult experiences but to soften the heart to fully experience life as it arises and passes.

Cultivation of the uplift of appreciative joy, for example, or the steadying of equanimity, helps you move toward abandonment of the entanglements and weariness of identification with what might be called *mine-ness*—the experience of attachment to self. The fullness of appreciative joy in any given moment, whether for another person or in experiencing the fragrance of a flower, is not dependent on attachments nor on what came before or after. Equanimity brings a spaciousness, enabling you to experience suffering, along with the balance needed to let go and graciously welcome new life as it emerges.[20]

Buddhist Meditation and Social Change

Vega-Frey tackles the question of whether social justice is built into vipassana and, if so, of whether it is a natural or even an intended outcome. In his own life, he is deeply committed to combatting societal racism and the construction of discrimination as it is supported by racist policy and authoritarian regime. He is involved in ethnic and racial justice work both at home in the United States as well as in Burma from afar, or from within when it is possible to travel and to engage there.

Yet while the projects of spiritual and social liberation may influence and inform each other, ultimately, they may not be the same. The

20. I am indebted to vipassana teachers, especially Stephen Smith, for expanding my understanding of the brahmaviharas, including at "Seeing Security Everywhere," an online retreat with Vipassana Hawai'i, June 11–20, 2021.

former is a guide to freedom from the tyranny of the mind, opening a way to pure love and compassion no matter what conditions you find yourself in. The latter is designed to change the conditions of society in which people live and grow. Developing your ability to be at peace with the changing conditions of the world does not in itself lead to the development of a just social structure. And the traditional processes of creating and enforcing more just social dynamics do not necessarily also develop the individual skills necessary to produce the inner liberation of mind. The processes of spiritual and social liberation work in different spheres.

Moreover, if we focus solely on changing the system, without seeking to develop our own equanimity or investigating the emotional and ethical motivation behind our engagement, we undermine our ability to awaken because our efforts are focused on the external causes of harm, at the expense of internal liberation from suffering. This can result in burn-out among societal activists.

On the other hand, those who focus on acceptance of any conditions without awareness and compassion for the external sources of that suffering, and without an ethical commitment to nonviolence and kindness, are potentially denying the possibility of shifting oppressive conditions that affect certain populations so much more deeply than others.

Important questions arise: If seclusion is necessary to achieve ultimate liberation in Buddhism, how effective can we be as engaged agents of social change? Is it a delusion to think we can have it all? If inner liberation of mind takes place in a different sphere than liberatory justice work in the world, to what extent can they be intertwined?

There is a delicate, dynamic dance between the individual effort of the self toward liberation of the cruelty of our own minds and collective systematic action within society toward liberation from the tyrannies of structural racism and sexism. Buddhists are discovering frameworks for justice work to create a healthy society that stem from outside of Buddhism, but are compatible with it. Michele and Jesse state that interfaith dialogue is an example of a framework that holds the possibility for helping to establish peace in Burma today. They are discovering that in the midst of violent clashes, interfaith relations have the potential to birth incremental understandings.[21]

The discussion surrounding Buddhist meditation and social change is alive within Buddhism, where challenges are arising in engagement with justice, particularly regarding awareness of racial bias. Meditation teachers who are Black and teach from Zen and Tibetan traditions are calling for a new, radical dharma that recognizes that a delusional view of reality and unsatisfactoriness within people's own minds should not be left to individuals to seek to alleviate alone, since these are reinforced by systematic oppressions in society.

For example, the three authors of *Radical Dharma* interweave Black prophetic tradition and theory with personal narratives of Buddhist practitioners. As Buddhism leads an individual toward the cessation of the ego, greater awareness, and the illumination of barriers in the mind and body, these authors see "the white superiority complex" as one such barrier. It is one that white Americans, and many Buddhist teachers and practitioners, live within. In response, they bring a radical challenge to Buddhism:

> At this time when the Dharma is needed more than ever—a time when our very existence is threatened as a result of our socially embedded greed, hatred, and ignorance—its expansive potential to liberate us from suffering is in danger of being rendered impotent because it is held in subjugation to the very systems that it must thoroughly examine.[22]

The authors argue that until ignorance of white supremacy and anti-Black racism is shattered, freedom from these conditions will

---

21. Vega-Frey and McDonald, interview.

22. Rev. angel Kyodo williams, Lama Rod Owens, and Jasmine Syedullah, *Radical Dharma: Talking Race, Love, and Liberation* (Berkeley, CA: North Atlantic Books, 2016), 19, Kindle.

never be possible. Rev. angel Kyodo williams calls "whiteness" a "social ego" that is identified with by white people as closely as they identify with their own name, yet they are unwilling to name this. This collective ego needs to be detached from along with the personal ego, as it is as "void of inherent identity as the personal ego."[23]

The authors of *Radical Dharma* recognize the need for quiet space in retreat. But they subvert the retreat's place as the space in which real insight is born. Insight, rather, emerges in direct engagement with the world, the true field of practice for sources of awakening. It is during retreat that integrative understanding can then be honed.[24]

What Do We Learn from Buddhism?

What can mindfulness learn from Buddhism? A few clarifications are needed before we can answer this question: (1) Buddhism is not just mindfulness; (2) Western mindfulness is not Buddhism; (3) even within a Western context, Buddhist practice always begins with ethical commitment; and (4) within Buddhism itself are arising the very criticisms we are leveling at mindfulness today—that we must wake up to the social ego as well as seek freedom from the personal ego.

Keeping these points in mind, mindfulness teachers and practitioners might draw from Buddhism the importance of struggling with our purpose as we engage in mindfulness practice. It is important to ask what character of liberation is possible or desireable for us. Is it primarily personal liberation from deluded forms of thought? Or liberation from a social ego deeply attached to a privileged racial identity (if applicable)? Or learning to achieve greater equanimity to ground us in the struggle for societal justice? If we do not ask these questions and engage in the struggle they present, we may inadvertently be reinforcing the dominant ways of being that are brought to us by a billion-plus-dollar mindfulness industry.

If mindfulness is part of your Buddhist practice, and you conclude

---

23. williams et al., 22.
24. williams et al., 24.

that your serious and primary purpose is liberation of the mind toward freedom from all attachments, that may be a form of contribution to compassion in the world as you detach from consumption and develop greater compassion for life.

One reason I continue to learn from teachers who are serious about continuing the tradition of their Burmese teachers is not because I am also beholden to this particular lineage. Rather, I see that what they are teaching is not simply geared toward adding a new mindful dimension to my life to make it a fuller, modern life. As I am doing through study of critical theory and theology and through feminist embodiment, I experience that through their teaching they are, at base, challenging the dominant construction of happiness in our culture. This process of taking ethical precepts seriously and practicing insight meditation pursues a path toward freedom that means letting go of cherished beliefs, possibly even some relationships, and participation in societal values. It is revolution, even guerilla warfare, and nothing less. Buddhist meditation teachers like Rev. williams and authors of *Radical Dharma* are taking that even further—challenging Buddhist and mindfulness teachers alike to deconstruct whiteness as a social ego.

I learn from Buddhist practice a tenderness with which the teachers approach both the self and the difficulty of this gradual awakening. It is skillful to take refuge in quiet, as well as to take breaks from it, and always to connect to community. The practice of lovingkindness is not just a practice of feeling good and being happy but accompanies the cultivation of compassion, joy of appreciation, and gracious equanimity.

I learn from Buddhist practice to be aware and awake to the *nature* of things as they are. If I only look at the way things appear to me ("what is"), I may see them from only my perspective, like how a person has been greedy and it has affected me. I find this distinction helpful, because seeing the nature of the way things are reveals how we often delude ourselves about this nature everywhere—even within ourselves. If I simply watch my perception of *what is*, which is the instruction most often given in mindfulness teachings, I can miss seeing this delusion in myself. This is a danger of mindfulness, that we may not see how we can grow in our personal practice yet remain unaware of our own privilege, if we are in any type of position of privilege.

Before I did the research for this book, I might have even said I was primarily a practitioner of vipassana Buddhism. I now see that it's much more complicated than that. I engage in the process of insight meditation, but always within the context of the ethics of the faith tradition in which I am situated: Christianity. Buddhism and Christianity are both about liberation, but they hold different concepts of liberation. One is liberation of mind, leading to breaking the cycle of birth and death. Once you are liberated in Buddhism, you are no longer reborn to a life of suffering. The other is, in progressive Christian understanding, participation in the liberatory promise of living with God through eternity, but equally of helping to bring about justice, mercy, and love on earth, as it is in heaven.

In the prophetic Christian tradition, insight into oppression and the promise of justice in neighborhoods, interfaith communities, and the society in which I dwell emerge through immersion in those worlds. It is then in retreat, whether an hour a day in my own home, a day away from the city, or a retreat setting where refuge is found, that I hone that awareness. I do this while gaining from the practices of another tradition: Buddhism. Vega-Frey made a similar distinction when he wrote, "As someone whose American indigenous ancestry is deep in the past generations, I have learned a great deal that I value from indigenous friends and mentors who are in more immediate contact with their traditions." He notes that he does not confuse these traditions with the Dhamma but approaches them as a student. "When I sit in the sweat lodge, I don't practice vipassanā: I pray. That is how I honor that lineage. That is what that ceremony is designed for."[25]

---

25. Vega-Frey, *Insurgent Heart*, loc. 2858, 2864 of 5895.

I do not conflate Buddhism with Christianity or other religions. I come to meditation with the ethic of love and service I hold central as a Christian. But when I practice vipassana I do not sit and pray. I meditate. And I am left with certain questions: As Christian social justice challenges dominate constructions of happiness in our culture, how can mindfulness tools assist us in this journey? And where might they fit alongside Christian practice? We will turn in a later chapter to the primary religion of my life and the practice of my ancestors. But first, there is much we can learn from other key contemplative traditions. There are many languages found within various religious and spiritual practices that inspire us toward outward compassion and higher consciousness. Each of them highlights compassion for the most vulnerable and gaining awareness of self, Divine, and others. Each is expressed in unique ways, containing particular practices and theologies not found in others, while encompassing resonant values that echo one another. These spiritual practices inform us along our journey toward liberation of self and society.

Chapter 8

Radical, Revolutionary Love: Contemplative Religious Practice

When we understand what it means to be thankful for every-thing and to see the inherent beauty in all things, then God will be pleased with us. . . . In order to please God, we must be people of service. . . . People of service are the people of presence.[1]

As with Buddhist insight meditation, there is much we can learn from other ancient practices of meditation. I have studied some, but more importantly I have been invited into sacred spaces through my interfaith work, which is where I gain deeper insight into various spiritual practices steeped in faith. Contemplative, liberatory theologies and practices are deep and vast and ancient. Yet they are not often talked about when you hear about mindfulness today. They are hidden to persons both inside and outside of religions. In this chapter, I simply offer you experiences that have touched me along this spiritual journey.

The Path of Radical Love—An Islamic Sufi Way

I spent several weeks on a tour of Turkey, learning about its history, culture, and architecture, as well as about Islam (focusing on Sufism,

---

1. Cemalnur Sargut, *Beauty and Light: Mystical Discourses by a Contemporary Female Sufi Master* (ed. Tehseen Thaver; trans. Cangüzel Zülfikar; Louisville, KY: Fons Vitae, 2017), 132.

which is Islamic mysticism). We began in Istanbul, where we stood in the magnificent Hagia Sofia, once a Christian church, then a Muslim mosque, then a museum (it has since again become a mosque). I looked up to see the relief of the Madonna and Child, where for hundreds of years she blessed Christians, Muslims, and tourists from her honored space in the massive overhead dome. We entered the caves of Cappadocia, where early Roman Christians fled and hid from imperial persecutors, leaving their spirit and stories emblazoned in intricate frescoes on the walls. We walked the stalls of merchants in Bursa, where the Silk Road ends and entered mosque after mosque filled with magnificent mosaics. We visited the Mevlâna Museum, which houses the shrine of Mevlâna Rumi, the great Sufi poet and mystic of the thirteenth century. Once inside, we heard hushed whispers as dozens of tourists and devotees paid their respects and stood in awe admiring the gold-embroidered brocade and masterful woodcarvings. We were honored with a private audience with Esin Çelebi Bayru, a granddaughter of Rumi twenty-two generations removed. I was beginning to understand the ways Sufism infused the life of many people in Turkey and around the world, even though gatherings that would allow individual Sufi masters to create centers and amass power were, at the time I visited, forbidden in Turkey.

Back in Istanbul, we arrived at Uskudar University and entered a concrete block university building, not unlike those I am familiar with at home. We climbed the stairs to find a classroom that would easily accommodate our group of thirty, along with some Turkish students who were eager to join us. The room was filled with rows of chairs, and a platform was set in front of the room. I stayed back as people entered, and when I saw there were a few spots open in the front row, I made my way up. Someone asked if we could sit closer to the stage, so we all moved our chairs forward. I had a true front-row seat in the classroom.

We rose as a woman in her sixties entered the back of the room and made her way to the platform. She was wearing earrings of white wreaths and a delicate gold-filagree pin on her tailored red, black, and white plaid blazer. I was captivated by her diminutive stature, easy movements, and enormous smile. Sheikha Cemalnur Sargut took her seat onstage and, after some small talk, began to teach. "Sufism is a living way, not a philosophy, not a religion, but a living way.... If there is some pain in your heart, you feel happiness with this pain. This is the philosophy. Because you know that everything comes from Allah. Everything comes from Allah. No other power, only Allah."[2]

For the next several hours we listened, asked questions, and listened again. She told us that when her daughter died, her mother asked her if she felt pain. She felt pain in her heart, but she also felt happiness. "Believe me I live in heaven," she said.[3] She referred to the Torah and the Quran and other holy books and pointed toward the ultimate gift to all people to live in what I can best describe as ultimate Presence.

I felt tears begin to form and roll down my cheeks, not five minutes after she began to speak. They continued for the next hour and a half. At the time I didn't know why. I later realized this was physically the closest I have come in my life to sitting in the presence of someone who has been described, and who I experienced, to be an enlightened teacher. A scholar of Sufism remarked to a colleague, "She is one of those people that you and I have read about in books our whole lives."[4] A Sheikha and Sufi master, she is the Turkish leader of the Rifa'i Sufi order and an accomplished teacher and author in the contemporary Islamic world.

Sheikha Cemalnur spoke English, occasionally helped by her Turkish translator. Someone in our group asked about the need to offer gratitude, and the concept of chosenness. "Aren't we all chosen?" Sheikha Cemalnur responded. And she went on to explain that we do not give thanks. "It is not us giving thanks," she said. "It is Allah who gives thanks through us."[5]

---

2. Cemalnur Sargut, teaching, Uskudar University, Istanbul, Turkey, October 10, 2019.

3. Sargut, teaching.

4. Sargut, *Beauty and Light*, 7.

5. Sargut, teaching.

It is Allah who gives thanks through us. I sensed my breath slow and
my body become still as a realization sank into my mind and heart.
This is not about me at all; this is about complete integration into
greater consciousness—within us and surrounding us. This is devotion and transparency steeped in faith.

Sheikha Cemalnur continued, explaining that this is not about us,
yet we are as fully alive as possible and filled with joy. We are able to
be with deep pain and great joy in every moment of every day, and no
reaction to any of it is ours alone. "We are nothing but we are everything at the same time. If we know how to be nothing, then we'll be
everything," she said.[6]

I have heard Allah described in Islam, and in Sufism, simply as
love. The energy of love, the great force behind all creation. Sheikha
Cemalnur confirmed this:

> Everything has Allah. [If you see a stone], you never believe [in]
> the stone, you believe [in] the Allah in it. And when you love
> somebody, you never love this body. You love the name of Allah
> in somebody. So, we understand that religion means love. The
> culture of love, we will go to love. Because my teacher teach[es]
> me how to love Allah and how to love people, how to accept
> people.[7]

I have heard Buddhist teachers speak of those who are nothing but
joy coupled with full awareness of suffering; I have heard people say
that of His Holiness the Dalai Lama. I had the privilege of seeing His
Holiness from a faraway section of an auditorium, where I recall him
listening to a choir of children whose families were exiled from Tibet.
I observed him stand up after they sang, walk to the choir, and step
toward each child one at a time, stopping to gaze in their eyes and gently hold each child's face, more than a dozen of them. And as he took
this precious time to be present with the children, and as time seemed

<hr />

6. Sargut, teaching.
7. Sargut, teaching.

to stop, his actions and demeanor were incongruous with the observable discomfort of the celebrities onstage with him, eager for their time to speak with him themselves. Although I was moved, I wasn't close enough that tears fell from the contagious spirit of that joy. But sitting at the feet of Sheikha Cemalnur they continued to spill from my eyes as emotions pulsed quietly through my body—tears of pain, one year after Ron died. Humbling tears, for the tremendous serendipity of coming on this trip and being here in this moment. Tears I didn't understand.

I finally worked up the courage to ask her a question about what it takes for a person to come to the fullness she was describing. My question centered on how to respond when, in my country, people tend to just pick a religion or practice that suits them, without any sense that there is anything required of them. She replied:

> If you love Allah, you have discipline. You have discipline because you understand you need the discipline, because you must do your work, you must wake up early. This is life. And when you wake up early, you feel happiness. Because you see the sun, the sun takes you to Allah. You see the sun. And if you do that once, [or] if you pray at night, how happy you are. Without telephone, without somebody coming, you and Allah together.[8]

Such wisdom for those of us never without our phone, never fully alone with God or the rising sun or the night stars. In Sufism, the heart awakens as it is fused with the Divine and extends to awakening within relationships with others. The love between people and the love between a person and God are metaphors for each other, intimately intertwined in Sufi writings. Omid Safi, professor of Islamic studies at Duke University and our tour guide in Turkey, suggests that one way to be in relationship and to greet one another would be to ask, "How is your heart doing at this very moment, at this breath?"[9]

---

8. Sargut, teaching.

9. See Omid Safi, "The Disease of Being Busy," *On Being*, November 6, 2014, https://onbeing.org/blog.

We normally ask, "How are you?" and the response usually turns from how we actually *are* to what we are *doing*. Professor Safi hears, as do I, a lot of "I'm so busy" when we ask "How are you?" on our university campuses. In fact, I often catch myself responding the same way when asked how I am. On today's academic campus, it is a kind of badge of honor and an expectation to be busy. Imagine if we asked, "How is your heart doing?" The question might open our hearts wider and elicit a very different answer.

Sufism is deeply relational in the sense that the focus is contemplation on radical love.[10] Radical love, a term drawn from the poetry of Rumi, refers to the Divine Light within each person. Spilling into the public square, radical love is also justice. Safi submits that as he reads the poetry of the mystics, from Rumi and his teachers and students to more recent writings, he realizes that the journey toward understanding is not an individual one but a collective one. Through discourses with a teacher like Sheikha Cemalnur, communities learn together.[11] It is a journey in which one discovers that humanity is but a reflection of Divine Love.

Contemplation on the poetry of the mystics and on the words of the Quran are deeply mindful practices for opening the heart and mind. Safi sees this deeper understanding in a poem by the Sufi master Rumi, where radical love is "overflowing, spilling-over love as one that mingles between God and humanity, humanity and humanity, this world and that world, here and there, now and forever":[12]

A Meditation: Contemplating Poetry

Look:
love mingles with Lovers

10. Omid Safi, *Radical Love: Teachings from the Islamic Mystical Tradition* (New Haven: Yale University Press, 2018).

11. Safi, *Radical Love*, xlix.

12. Safi, *Radical Love*, xxv.

> See:
> spirit mingling with body
>
> How long will you see life
> as "this"
> and "that"?
>
> "Good"
> and "bad"?
>
> Look at how this
> and that
> are mingled.[13]

The Sufi path is one of discipline of mind and heart, toward understanding we are nothing but we are everything at the same time. If we know how to be nothing, then we'll be everything. Sufism is uniquely born of faithful devotees within Islam. Yet the understanding of the interconnectedness, the oneness of humanity encompassed within the Divine, and the Divine within humanity, also emanates in a different language from a vastly different tradition, that of Sikhism.

Revolutionary Love—A Pathway Born from Sikhism

"Go to the places of pain." Valarie Kaur's words echoed throughout the beautiful auditorium— filled with attentive students and their families—of the new Musco Center for the Arts at Chapman University. I had invited her to speak for our annual baccalaureate service, a spiritual send-off for our graduating students. Kaur told the graduates the story of hearing of the death of a friend she revered as an uncle, and whom she called Balbir Uncle. Balbir Singh Sodhi was the first person killed in a hate crime following the attack on the Twin

---

13. Excerpt from Rumi, "Mingling," in Safi, *Radical Love,* xxvi. Used by permission.

Towers of the World Trade Center in New York City on 9/11. He was standing in front of his gas station in Mesa, Arizona, about to plant a new pack of flowers, when a gunman drove by in his pickup truck and slowed down just long enough to shoot him five times in the back, killing Balbir instantly.

I sat on the stage gazing through the tears in my eyes toward her captivated audience. There was silence and expectation in the auditorium as Valarie continued. She told the students about going to meet his family, and eventually his widow, in his native country of India. At the time, Kaur was traveling throughout the world with a camera, documenting experiences of grief following growing numbers of tragic bias-related violence against Sikhs. When they met, Valarie asked Balbir's wife: "What would you like to say to the people of America?" And then she shared how stunned she was at the response. She expected to hear words of anger, but Balbir Uncle's widow said to tell them "Thank you."[14] She wanted to convey her gratitude to the people of all faiths who showed her so much love when she came to the United States following her husband's murder.

Just as I, growing up in the United States, you may know little about Sikhism. The Sikh understanding of service and devotion begins with Guru Nanak. Revered as the first guru of Sikhism in the early sixteenth century, he became enlightened at the young age of thirty. His enlightenment brought him awareness of the nature of reality—including that human beings could become aware of the divine light within everyone and understand the oneness of all.

The tenth guru, Guru Gobind Singh, established The Order of the Khalsa, the community of Sikhs, who are both a meditative and a warrior people willing to defend themselves and people from any religion or culture under threat of tyranny and injustice. Guru Gobind Singh instituted among other sacred practices and articles *kesh*, or unshorn hair. Sikhs wore the turban, which for them is a sign of

---

14. Valarie Kaur, Chapman University Interfaith Baccalaureate Service Address, Orange, CA, May 20, 2016, https://www.chapman.edu/fic.

equality among all people as well as a commitment to service. Today, wearing a turban makes the Sikh wearer visible in case anyone is in need. Hence, the appalling irony that the turban came to signify a person who should be feared and targeted as a terrorist after 9/11, leading to terrible tragedies like Balbir Singh Sodhi's murder, along with too many others killed by white extremists.

My dear friends Bicky and Gurpreet Singh and Jasdeep Singh Mann have introduced me and my friends, colleagues, and students at Chapman University to Sikhs from around the world. They have invited us into their homes for meals, into their gudwara (Sikh place of worship and gathering), and to activities of the Sikh community throughout southern California. Gagandeep Kaur Mann and Chai Seng Saechao even invited me to bring students to their wedding ceremony, which took place at a gudwara, where we participated in hours of traditions, ceremonies, festivities, and shared meals.

Perhaps one of the most memorable experiences I have had was the honor of helping—along with the Sikh community, various Boy Scout troops, and random volunteers—to join in hours of placing dainty flower petals on a Sikh float for the annual Rose Bowl Parade in Pasadena, California. The Sikh community views having a float as an opportunity to get their message of love for all humankind out to millions of people each year. As if the thousands of volunteer hours building the massive float were not enough, the Sikh community chose to serve even more. In the parking lot of the enormous warehouse where dozens of floats were under construction, members of the Sikh community prepared and served *langar* (a vegetarian meal freely offered to the community in places around the world) for the hundreds of volunteers working daily on the other floats. Students at Chapman University were inspired by their *seva*, or service, when members of the Sikh community invited them into their homes to stay during the Parliament of the World's Religions in Toronto in 2018. This, along with receiving free *langar* served daily to the thousands of international guests, are among their most cherished memories of attending the Parliament.

Kaur's book *See No Stranger* offers guidance for these times of devastating division, guidance born from Sikh stories and her own experience. Kaur begins with how to love others. The first step is *wonder*, which she learned from Papa Ji, her grandfather, while growing up on the family farm and hearing his stories filled with Sikh wisdom. She would hear him continually humming the poetic words of Guru Nanak he memorized from *Sri Guru Granth Sahib*. This sacred canon of the Sikh faith is comprised of poems called *shabads*, which are recited or set to music. The *shabads* Kaur heard included words of wonder about fire, colors, animals, wind, and water. Kaur writes,

> When Papa Ji was humming the *shabads* day and night, he was not praying as much as practicing a constant communion with all things. . . .
> "Waheguru, Waheguru!" Papa Ji would say. It was our word for God, but he would say it throughout the day like it was a deep breath. "Wahe" is an expression of awe, and "guru" is the light that dispels darkness. So even God's name was an expression of wonder at the divine around us and within us.[15]

Papa Ji taught her to wonder in a way Kaur sees as central to many traditions. He taught her to look on anyone or anything and say, "You are a part of me I do not yet know."[16]

Kaur introduces the concept of *revolutionary love*, which includes relating to the other, to our opponents, and to ourselves. In her raw and beautiful personal narrative, Kaur starts by offering ways of being in relationship with others who are different from ourselves. Her process begins with *loving others*, which includes the importance not only of wonder but of grieving, and at times resistance or fighting. She draws on stories of the woman warrior, the princess warrior, who

---

15. Valarie Kaur, *See No Stranger: A Memoir and Manifesto of Revolutionary Love* (New York: Random House, 2020), 9.
16. Kaur, *See No Stranger,* 11.

is also the wise woman in Sikh history and lore. Then Kaur turns her attention to an even more difficult process: learning to *love opponents*. This includes allowing space and time for raging against, then listening to, and then reimagining with opponents. Rage is processed in safe containers where our body's impulses can be expressed without harm and without shame. Here is how Kaur coaches you to find a safe container, and then to ask yourself questions about your rage:

> Safe containers take many forms: shaking, weeping, venting, writing, art, music, dance, drama, meditation, trauma therapies, rituals, and ceremonies of all kinds. Only when we give rage an external expression outside our bodies can we be in relationship to it. We can then ask: "What information does my rage carry? What is it telling me? How do I want to harness this energy?"[17]

Kaur admits she found herself going to the places of pain, throwing herself into travel and film documentaries in spaces of tragedy, before learning about a third component of revolutionary love: *loving ourselves*. She has since fully embraced the importance of caring for herself, and offers a pathway to love yourself using the birthing metaphor of pausing to breathe, pushing as one endures pain, and transitioning as one births and embraces new life. Activists, she submits, must learn mindful techniques of caring for self along the collective path of caring for others.

Kaur shares a meditation, a spiritual training, which she has developed for herself. This practice is one of opening to wonder and curiosity about "what is" rather than about "what we think is." This helps us to recognize our own unconscious bias. Repeat to yourself, as you see persons and animals on the streets and in the news, "You are a part of me I do not yet know."[18]

---

17. Kaur, *See No Stranger*, 131.
18. Kaur, *See No Stranger*, 27, adapted with permission.

Meditation: You Are a Part of Me I Do Not Yet Know
When you see another person, whether you are walking about or watching a screen, say *Sister. Brother. Sibling. Aunt. Uncle.* You can do this with animals and parts of the earth as well, seeing them as part of *us* rather than as *them.* Say in your mind as you see them, *You are a part of me I do not yet know.*

What is clearly present in these ancient practices is the depth of compassion that is the heart and core of the canon of poetry and scripture from whence they grew and flourished. Other mystical traditions also draw on this deep well of compassion. Within Judaism, this is intertwined with the foundational notion of *hospitality* to the stranger as service to the Divine. Some are finding it useful to incorporate classical mindfulness tools to access this well of compassion and interconnection.

Love and Justice in Jewish Mindfulness

There are many more traditions that include silent contemplative practices for opening the heart. Some of these mystical traditions are incorporating mindfulness tools, which makes them clear and accessible to people in those traditions today—Jewish mindfulness is an excellent example. Many years ago, I was director of a campus ministry that operated out of the Koinonia House (K-House), a former sorority house over a century old in the middle of the Washington State University campus. Before I had heard of mindfulness, and when many of us were just beginning forays into interfaith dialogue, I was privileged to be in this space that was ahead of its time. Even before I arrived, the Jewish community from the area held its Shabbat services in the K-House, which was an ecumenical Christian campus ministry building. The Jewish community was not served by a regular rabbi, so they at times invited one when the opportunity arose. On one occasion, I joined them to hear a rabbi who today might be said to be practicing Jewish mindfulness, but at the time was simply following a mystic, meditative strain of Judaism.

The rabbi asked the Jewish community if they could speak the name of God, but she was met with silence. She next suggested they whisper it. Even then, I sat with the congregation as they kept silence. She knew that in Judaism the name of God is commonly written with the consonants YHVH (without vowels) and held in such reverence that it is never spoken. "Ok, breathe it," the rabbi finally suggested. She demonstrated, and her breathing sounded like a whisper of *hay* (Hebrew for the letter H) with the inbreath, and *hay* again with the outbreath. The breath of God is the breath of life. The creation story in Genesis relays that God formed the human out of dust and blew the breath of life into the human, who then became a living being.

Drawing on this notion that the letter H is connected to the breath of God from which life springs forth as well as to the sound of breath, Jewish mindfulness today can include the contemplative practice of "YHVH breathing." In Jewish mysticism, these letters correspond to the nothingness before the arising of anything (*yud*), the sound of breath (*hay*), and the fullness of everything (*vav*). One may begin repeating *yud* before each breath, inhale *hay*, pause for *vav*, and exhale *hay*, or substitute the Hebrew letters with the words *empty, in, full, out* for this breath meditation.[19] Jewish mindfulness is said to be helpful for awakening the self to new realizations but also to inspire care for others.[20] It awakens mindful, loving attention. "The present moment of experience" is equated in this practice to the "Divine manifesting as the Present Moment of Being."[21]

---

19. Jeff Roth, *Me, Myself & God: A Theology of Mindfulness* (Woodstock, VT: Jewish Lights Publishing, 2016), 33–45; also see a full description of YHVH breathing and other Jewish contemplative practices in the Appendix.

20. See Jonathan Feiner, *Mindfulness: A Jewish Approach* (Los Angeles, CA: Mosaica Press, 2020), 64–65.

21. Roth, *Me, Myself & God*, xvii.

Shortly after I became dean of the chapel at Chapman University, I was asked by Marilyn Harran, director of the Rodgers Center for Holocaust Education, whether I would be willing to interview Elie Wiesel, a Holocaust survivor who was awarded the Nobel Peace Prize in 1986 for his work combatting violence and racism. Wiesel was a person whose life and work embodied both interiority and activism. He wrote about topics like silence and transcendence and was engaging in work combating genocide throughout the globe.

Wiesel would be coming to Chapman for a week and would address large questions—each day interviewed by a different professor or dean at the university. The topic for our day surrounded the question "Why Believe?" I was honored to be asked—and I was terrified. He was a giant, and the question was even bigger. I began to prepare, and to overprepare, reading everything I could find he had written on the subject. I even reread *Night*—last having set eyes on it in my high school days.[22]

What I recall, sitting on the stage in the beautiful Fish Interfaith Center that day, was the sense that I was sitting in a place of honor, completely engulfed in Presence. If I had not been in front of an audience and tasked to keep track of time, I would have completely forgotten there was such a thing as time at all. What I do recall of Wiesel's answers to my questions and of our dialogue was his insistence that if you ever meet someone who claims they know who God is, walk the other way. For no human fully knows.

That meeting occurred the year I was involved in a course at UCLA to become certified as a facilitator of mindfulness. The interview with Wiesel fell during one of the in-person days of a four-day intensive gathering we had periodically throughout the year. I received permission to come late that day, so after my interview with Wiesel, I hopped in the car and drove into Los Angeles. I entered the classroom still wearing my business suit and heels, and immediately felt out of

---

22. Elie Wiesel, *Night* (trans. Marion Wiesel; New York: Hill and Wang, 1956, 2006).

place in the casual crowd. That afternoon, when I had an opportunity during an open dialogue with some classmates to mention I had met Elie Wiesel, my comment was met with flatness. It was either because my ego was swelling after I had just met and sat on stage with him and he spoke with me, or it was because he wasn't known or held in high esteem. I suspect it was heavily the former—my ego bursting at the seams. I came to realize that I can be in the present moment in a pure sense at one point, and then in the next moment I consider the experience *mine* and want to hold onto and highlight it. This is our journey, as we ask over and over, for whom do we do this practice?

Intertwining Mindfulness and Religion toward Liberation

These are but a few examples that have offered me moments of presence and opened my heart to see that deeper ways of living in presence are found within these ancient paths and are being lived out today. Many pathways, committed to an ethics of global justice and mindful discipline and practice, are not only hidden from today's mindfulness movement in the West but often from many who practice the very religions they stem from. Yet here we find the power of contemplation igniting compassion and rare, radical, revolutionary love, toward transformation. These practices are more likely to disrupt rather than support the purposes and goals of self-interested individuals, institutions, and communities.

These pathways toward justice are all different. They emerge from the examples of enlightened individuals who came or are coming to awakening through distinct stories, scriptures, prayer, meditation, and discipleship. What they have in common is the practitioner's heart of compassion and dedication to a life filled with an ethic of intentional service, discipline, and devotion. In Sufism, this minimally includes the disciplines of fasting, prayer, teaching, studying, and learning in relationship to others. For Sikhism, this means going to the places of pain where one can be of service to those in need. Within these pathways, already embedded, are unique mindful practices of presence. And some are finding classical mindfulness tools to be an important addition to the practices of their own faith tradition. Bringing classical mindfulness tools into other religious or spiritual traditions may provide contemporary and accessible ways to further awaken the heart with compassion.

I have witnessed many more persons exhibiting humility born of devotion and dedication to their specific contemplative or spiritual practices and found bridges of peace emerging among additional Muslim, Jewish, and more communities such as Baha'i, Hindu, and the Church of Jesus Christ of Latter-day Saints. For a longer investigation, we turn now to the tradition of my ancestors and life, Christianity. We learn from two streams that have emerged within Christianity: contemplative practice and liberation theologies.

CHAPTER 9

Centering Prayer in Christianity

We're mindful because there's something in us that's deeply, mystically stabilized enough that God remembers through us.[1]

"At this point in my life," Pastor Ben said, "I do not go seeking. Whatever comes to me, I consider, and if I agree, 'whatever comes to me, goes through me.' It is not for me. It is through me."[2]

I felt my breathing slow as I let Ben's words sink in, dropping into stillness and quiet. Sitting on a couch next to my sister in a diverse, middle-class neighborhood in Indianapolis, I realized this was wisdom articulated in a way I had heard before, first on the Big Island of Hawaii from a meditation teacher and wise elder. The next time it was sitting in an apartment in Idaho with an enlightened Episcopal friend facing the end of her life who had just arrived from the Greek island of Corfu. Later, I heard similar words from another tradition entirely, as Sheikha Cemalnur Sargut explained that it is not I who give thanks, it is Allah giving thanks through me. Each of these times, what I heard is the wisdom of living with transparency. And what I learned in these settings is that there are various understandings of devotion, each through unique and different practices like meditation and prayer, which enable healing to occur *through* people, as they allow themselves to mirror the Divine in the world.

Ready for a mental break after some months of travel and research

---

1. Cynthia Bourgeault, interview by author, November 27, 2019.
2. Rev. Ben Keckler, book study, Indianapolis, IN, November 6, 2019.

for this book, I was visiting my sister Jane and her husband, Steve, in Indianapolis. I accompanied them to a book study at the home of their former pastor who, like them, had recently retired to the neighborhood. It was a chilly autumn evening. We were welcomed into the warmth of the living room. A dozen members from their church greeted us, and we settled on a couch and chairs lining the room. A wood fire in a brick fireplace blazed at one end, casting a warm glow on our conversation.

Pastor Ben began by inviting each member to answer one of the reflection questions posed at the close of the book chapters assigned for the day. He offered his reflection on Diane Millis's notion in *Conversation—The Sacred Art* of what it means to discover the calling of our hearts, which she calls a "divine thread, a thread of meaning and purpose, a calling."[3] Millis writes:

> Following a path with heart invites and challenges each of us to strike a fine balance between inward listening to our hearts and outward, socially engaged listening with our hearts to the realities of the world in which we live. If the path I am considering taking seems to benefit only me, and not my family or community, then it's probably all about me. If a path truly has heart, it will enhance real communion and benefit others in our community and beyond.[4]

Discerning a "path with heart" is central to Christian contemplative traditions. On this path, one is true *to* oneself but not *for* oneself, travels as an individual but on behalf of the community, and is acting but reveals God acting *through* one at the same time. This path is discerned in silence, in contemplative prayer. Centering Prayer, the closest practice to mindfulness today that we find within Christianity, is one vehicle for this discovery.

---

3. Diane M. Millis, *Conversation—The Sacred Art: Practicing Presence in an Age of Distraction* (Woodstock, VT: SkyLight Paths), loc. 1001 of 2250. Kindle.

4. Millis, *Conversation*, loc. 978 of 2250.

What Is Centering Prayer?

Centering Prayer was pioneered in the late twentieth century by Father Thomas Keating, a Cistercian priest, monk, and abbot at St. Benedict's Trappist Monastery in Snowmass, Colorado, and was built on a long tradition of similar practices.[5] Some of the best-known writings on this type of prayer available to us today include those of St. Teresa of Ávila and St. John of the Cross, writing in Spain in the fifteenth and sixteenth centuries, respectively.

Teresa of Ávila calls the practice of silent prayer "prayer of the quiet." She encourages her readers to be gentle when thoughts arise, to stop analyzing the experience, and simply allow even a moment of stillness to occur. She writes:

> The soul shouldn't try to analyze the state she's in; it is a gift given to the will, not the intellect. Let the soul enjoy it without any effort beyond a few loving words. Even if you are not actively trying to keep yourself from thinking in this state, thoughts often cease by themselves here, at least for a moment.[6]

The title of her work *The Interior Castle* suggests movement inward, to rest in precious space. Centering Prayer includes awareness of the body as well. The medieval mystics saw the body as a distraction, yet they also understood it as a way to immediately sense God's presence. This required an awareness of body—not just noticing comfort or discomfort but enjoying simple aspects of life that are only experienced through the senses and body.[7]

In Centering Prayer, you choose a word that is meaningful to you and repeat it with each breath. A simple formula for remembering

---

5. Thomas Keating, *Open Mind, Open Heart: The Contemplative Dimension of the Gospel* (New York: Continuum, 1996), chapter 3.

6. Teresa of Ávila, *The Interior Castle* (trans. Mirabai Starr; New York: Berkley Publishing Group, 2003), 108.

7. Stefan Gillow Reynolds, *Living with the Mind of Christ: Mindfulness and Christian Spirituality* (London: Darton, Longman & Todd, 2016), loc. 1025 of 4850, Kindle.

how to relate to your thoughts in Centering Prayer is presented by Cynthia Bourgeault, a contemporary teacher of Centering Prayer: "Resist no thought, Retain no thought, React to no thought, Return ever so gently to the sacred word."[8] The anonymous fourteenth-century author of *The Cloud of Unknowing* describes this practice, and notes:

> This word will be your defense in conflict and in peace.... Should some thought go on annoying you demanding to know what you are doing, answer with this one word alone. If your mind begins to intellectualize over the meaning and connotations of this little word, remind yourself that its value lies in its simplicity. Do this and I assure you these thoughts will vanish. Why? Because you have refused to develop them with arguing.[9]

This description of a person's relationship with his or her thoughts as engaging in argument is, in my experience, wonderfully accurate! In Centering Prayer, as in mindfulness, the understanding that your thoughts are just that—thoughts that may or may not be true—is central. If you find you are caught up in thinking and a busy mind, not to worry. I often heard Father Keating reminding people to return to their chosen word when their mind wandered, and if it did so often, how wonderful; they had a thousand opportunities to return to God!

To be honest, I admit that I find mindfulness meditation easier to practice, perhaps because there is a physical sensation to return to (breath or body awareness) and because in mindfulness a certain "investigating" of your thoughts is permissible before returning to that sensation. I know from conversations with others that I am not alone in this, which may be another reason for the appeal of mindfulness today. In Centering Prayer, you are simply invited to let go, and

---

8. Cynthia Bourgeault, *The Heart of Centering Prayer: Nondual Christianity in Theory and Practice* (Boulder, CO: Shambala, 2016), 32.

9. William Johnston, ed., *The Cloud of Unknowing and the Book of Privy Counseling* (New York: Image Books, 1973), 48.

return. Let go, and return. Let go, and return. Perhaps I need more instruction than that!

Yet, as valuable as I find the actual practice of mindfulness, I curiously find myself returning to Centering Prayer. As soon as the coronavirus epidemic began, I discovered I had stopped beginning my meditation with attention to mindful breath or a body scan and was silently repeating a sacred word I had chosen some forty years ago. There is something deeper that I need that is held in the prayer.

To engage in Centering Prayer, take some time before you begin, and experiment with words to find one that feels like home or opens a welcoming space when you repeat it but is without layers of meaning. A word that is like taking a deep, relaxing breath. A word that serves, as Bourgeault notes, "as the symbol of your willingness to consent to God's presence and action within."[10] It will serve as a touchpoint to return to that gently enables you to let go of rational faculties. I like two-syllable words so they can be repeated with the inhale and exhale of each breath in mediation. It might be a sacred word, like *Divine*, *Spirit*, or *Jesus*. It might be a word like *loving* or *alive* or *aware*. Don't overthink this—you can always choose a different word later.

Practice of Centering Prayer
- Choose a word that speaks to you, a symbol indicating your willingness to open yourself to the action of God's presence within you.
- Once you have found your word, find a quiet spot where you can sit upright, yet comfortably. Close your eyes.
- Begin to repeat your sacred word silently to yourself. As you become aware of a thought, simply allow that thought to fade, and continue repeating your word. Similarly, as soon as you notice a sound, or sense an emotion, or feel any physical sensation, come back to mentally touch the word gently. After you

---

10. Bourgeault, *The Heart of Centering Prayer*, 29.

> engage in this process for a bit, you may find the word drops out, and you are simply sitting quietly.
> • At the end of this prayer period, remain in silence a few moments, then open your eyes.

Insight Meditation and Centering Prayer

I began my six-month spiritual pilgrimage to study mindfulness with a five-day silent vipassana retreat. I chose this particular retreat for three reasons: it started the week I was beginning my sabbatical, and I knew I needed to be forced to turn off my cell phone and close down my email in order to sever myself from my normal workday. Second, it was in Hawaii, which needs no explanation! And third, I wanted to interview vipassana teachers Michele McDonald and Jesse Maceo Vega-Frey, who reside in Hawaii.

So off I flew to the isle of Oahu, to attend a silent retreat prior to meeting with Michele and Jesse on the Big Island. I was still deeply grieving Ron, my long-time partner who had died of heart disease less than a year before. I had not attempted a silent retreat since then, knowing that being alone with my thoughts and emotions might just be too intense with my heart still tender from the pain of losing him. This was my first attempt to enter days of silence in well over a year. I arrived my second day in Hawaii at the Kahumani Organic Farms & Café, located several hours north of Honolulu. It was beautiful, green, and surrounded by lush hills. We ate delicious, nutritious, organic food grown and raised on the property. It was also hot, humid, swarming with mosquitos, and lacking air conditioning. There was a swimming pool, so for a short time each day, if we remained alone and silent, we could slip in for some relief. Oh, and a rooster had taken up residence right under my small bunk room in the residential lodge, letting me know before dawn in no uncertain terms when it was time to rise. The setting offered a perfect opportunity to practice staying present through both comfort and discomfort!

Vipassana retreats are normally scheduled so the retreatants do not speak, except during short interviews with a teacher every other day. Each evening, the teacher offers a dhamma talk, offering insight into the practice. Retreatants spend each day following a relatively strict schedule, alternating between sitting and walking meditations throughout the day, interspersed with meals and sometimes a daily assigned job such as washing dishes. Students begin by accepting the Buddhist ethical precepts: refraining from killing living beings; refraining from taking what is not freely offered to us; not engaging in sexual activity; not imbibing intoxicants or engaging in addictive behaviors; and extending lovingkindness to all living beings (including insects and our fellow yogis, no matter how irritating). And we commit ourselves to forgo all distractions to practice—no texting, no email, no conversations, no writing, no reading, no surfing the web or social media, no Netflix, no alcohol, no interacting with the people dearest to you, no serious exercise routines, and no driving. All that's left is what you bring with you within your mind. Sure enough, in the silence and alone with my thoughts, by only the second day of this retreat I began to weep tears of grief, missing Ron. I wept through walking meditations, sitting meditations, rest periods, meals, and through the night.

On the third morning, I entered the top floor of a rustic, wood-beamed lodge for my first interview with our teacher, Mary Grace Orr, who is a Christian and a teacher of Buddhist insight meditation. I began by telling her that every author she mentioned in her evening dhamma talks were ones I was familiar with, including contemplatives within the Christian tradition. Once she learned my story, she commented that I was perhaps the only other vipassana practitioner and mindfulness teacher she had met who, like her, took my Christian roots seriously. I was surprised; surely others have felt the pull of both? I have interviewed others who have since then, but, truly, I have not met a lot of people openly claiming both—which is, in part, why I offer this book.

Then I shared the pain I felt, telling her, "It's as though I am sitting in a pool of tears." She affirmed my experience and essentially said to keep it up, saying something like: *now you know what it feels like to be present with suffering, and to sit in a pool of tears.* Gradually my tears subsided. I became curious about this teacher who understood the central role of suffering for Buddhism but also within Christianity.[11] In Buddhism, the First Noble Truth reveals that there is suffering, and that all beings experience it. It is through coming to understand suffering that liberation is achieved. Christianity also recognizes the inevitability of suffering in the lives of human beings. It is necessary—not in the sense that God wills particular suffering to specific individuals, but it is the space in which we come to let go of our control and begin to experience transformation. Understanding that Jesus suffered at the hands of the empire all the way to his death, Christians know that he accompanies and dwells with all who suffer. On the week following our retreat, Mary Grace graciously invited me for a personal tour of Hawai'i Volcanoes National Park, where she spent many hours as a volunteer. One overcast afternoon, we drove to a number of lookouts and stepped out of her dusty four-wheel-drive vehicle into the rain to take in magnificent views of the vast, flowing brown and grey ribboned landscape, which had been formed by lava flows. But before our tour of the park, I met my new teacher at her home, and she recounted her story.

Two years before I met her, Mary Grace had been in an automobile accident and had to undergo surgery. At the same time, her husband had to leave suddenly to travel away from home when his father died. She found herself alone and facing a difficult physical recovery. She realized at that moment that sitting in mindfulness meditation was not enough. She recalls:

> I went to sit one morning, and I sat down, had my Buddha image over there and I thought: I don't want to do this, I don't want

---

11. For a discussion of the experience and meaning of suffering in light of Christian theology, see chapter 5, "Living with Suffering," in Gail J. Stearns, *Open Your Eyes: Toward Living More Deeply in the Present* (Eugene, OR: Wipf & Stock, 2011), 63–77.

to do this, I want "The Lord is my shepherd I shall not want." I want something . . . that has a *you* to it. . . . That's what started it, and one thing led to another, and it's really been amazing.[12]

Since then, Mary Grace has reclaimed her Christian roots in her meditation practice. She has taken a deep dive into contemplative practice in the Christian mystical tradition and studied with Richard Rohr, Franciscan priest and teacher of Christian contemplation.[13]

Over thirty years ago, researchers concluded that Christian prayer and insight meditation can be combined. They introduced a practice called "Christian Insight Meditation," vipassana meditation practiced within a Christian understanding, meditation they compared to that presented by St. John of the Cross.[14] The process of learning Christian Insight Meditation developed those years ago precisely mirrors vipassana retreats offered throughout the country today. Christian teachers even cohosted a retreat with Rebecca Bradshaw, a teacher of insight meditation trained in the Buddhist tradition who was mentor to me throughout my year of mindfulness facilitation training at UCLA and with whom I have sat in silent retreats for up to two weeks at a time.

As we have seen, vipassana, or insight meditation, stems from a tradition that is complex and beautiful, infused with particular ethical precepts and values. For Mary Grace Orr, the practice of vipassana alongside exploration of Christian meditation is a fascinating journey. She shares with me that she continues to navigate what it means to claim both, as she finds the richness and resonance in each tradition.

For our purposes, I am interested in the integration of classical mindfulness tools, not of vipassana Buddhism itself, with the values

---

12. Mary Grace Orr, interview with author, Volcano, HI, July 9, 2019.

13. "Living School" Program, Center for Action and Contemplation, https://cac.org.

14. Kevin G. Culligan, Mary Jo Meadow, and Daniel Chowning, *Purifying the Heart: Buddhist Insight Meditation for Christians* (New York: Crossroad, 1994), 53, 58.

of the Christian contemplative tradition. I believe that for Christians, mindfulness tools can sharpen our meditation, while values stemming from following the way of Jesus undergird our practice.

Contemplative Prayer and Mindfulness Tools

Similarities between the practice of Christian contemplative tradition and mindfulness can be quite striking. Teresa of Ávila writes, "I used to be tormented by this turmoil of thoughts. A little over four years ago I came to realize by experience that thinking is not the same as mindfulness."[15] She comments that some people believe everything that pops into their minds, which is a dangerous delusion. Her description of mindfulness is surprisingly similar to the experience of practicing mindfulness today. She describes how at times during this prayer the mind can be on many things, but, as she suggests, "It could be that the soul is fully present with him in the innermost chamber while the mind stays on the periphery of the palace. . . ."[16] She assures the reader that even when the mind is busy, the soul can be at rest with God. She describes this further:

> Can we stop the stars from hurtling across the heavens? No. We cannot stop the mind, either. Off it goes, and then we send all the faculties after it. We end up thinking we are lost and blaming ourselves for wasting precious time in the presence of God. . . . The truth is, all this turmoil does not hinder my prayer or interfere with what I am trying to say. Instead, my soul is whole within its quietude, its love, its longing, and its clarity of consciousness.[17]

Teresa of Ávila's assurances bring to mind those offered by a mindfulness teacher when you experience what some call the "monkey

---

15. Teresa of Ávila, *The Interior Castle*, 91.
16. Teresa of Ávila, *The Interior Castle*, 92.
17. Teresa of Ávila, *The Interior Castle*, 92–93.

mind" jumping all around. In mindfulness, you are encouraged to notice your thoughts, then let them go and gently return to your breath. The more thoughts you have, the more often you have the opportunity to be mindful of them and return to the breath, or in the case of Centering Prayer, to God.

In a Christian mindfulness meditation, you begin by synchronizing breath with a sacred word. Breath is sacred. In the creation story of the Hebrew Bible, the Christian Old Testament, God breathes life into humanity. This meditation centers you within that vast Breath and brings your attention to center in this moment, in Presence. As you do this practice, each time your attention becomes distracted and you notice your mind has wandered, gently reintroduce your word to your mind and rest your inner attention on your breath. Begin with the intention to center in the present and Presence, with a sense of devotion, respect, and dignity. Try this for ten to twenty minutes, or if you choose just five minutes, adding another minute or two each time you practice. Be gentle with yourself. If you choose a two-syllable word, repeat one syllable with each inbreath and outbreath; if you choose a single syllable word, repeat the word with each breath.

A Christian Mindfulness Meditation

1. Choose a word that feels like "home," that brings you back to your center when you repeat it.
2. Sit in a comfortable position, alert but not rigid. Close your eyes if it is comfortable, or gently rest your gaze in front of you.
3. Bring attention to your breath. Repeat your chosen word with each breath. Let your mind "keep busy" with the word, while your inner attention rests on the sensation of your breath.
4. Take notice of where your attention on the breath rests most naturally in your body. Become aware of the sensations of inhaling, the sensations of exhaling, and the pauses in between. Watch an entire breath, then another, and another. Notice the coolness and warmth of your breath, the expansion and contraction of your body, the rising and falling of your abdomen, etc.

Continue to repeat your word. If you find you are caught in thought, recall your word and allow your mind to rest upon it, synchronizing your word with each breath. If it falls away just let it go. Allow yourself to simply rest here, open to a wider awareness of pure Presence within you.

Characteristics of Centering Prayer

If we are to incorporate mindfulness tools into a Christian practice of mindfulness, it is helpful to understand what aspects of Centering Prayer or Christian meditation are not found in classical mindfulness. I identify three elements: *intention*, *devotion*, and *transparency*.

Intention

Centering Prayer is done primarily with the intention toward openness to the movement of the Spirit rather than solely with attention, as one might prioritize in classical mindfulness. Bourgeault writes that Centering Prayer involves the cultivation of two qualities of the "release of attention." The first has been referred to within Christianity as *attention of the heart*. The second has, until now, not been identified specifically within Christian tradition. She notes that it may be what is referred to in Tibetan Buddhism as *objectless awareness*.[18] In my estimation, an analogy for the experience itself involves what Diana Winston describes in *The Little Book of Being* as "natural awareness." This way of being is one where your attention is on the awareness itself rather than all that the mind wants to focus on. Winston describes this experience as "generally relaxed, effortless, and spacious."[19]

In Centering Prayer, you enter with an intention, so in that sense, there is an agenda that is not present in "natural awareness." But the

---

18. Bourgeault, *The Heart of Centering Prayer*, 2.

19. Diana Winston, *The Little Book of Being* (Boulder, CO: Sounds True Publishing), 12, 20.

intention is one that only motivates you to the act of meditation, not one that dominates the experience of the prayer. Bourgeault writes, Once one is able to rest in a river of "pure awareness" even for nano-seconds, "bit by bit you'll discover that this inner spaciousness is no longer 'a place you go to' but 'a place you *come from*.'"[20] Sitting in silence leads to moments of dropping the repetition of your word, releasing thought to open awareness.

For Christians, this "place you come from" is God. The word "God" is a stumbling block for many, however, as it can conjure up images of an all-knowing, controlling, human-like being. But in the contempla-tive experience, God is both an experience and a concept of mystery greater than one person can wrap up in a neat definition, and impos-sible for a human mind to fully grasp or define. As Celtic scholar John Phillip Newell notes, "One of the problems with the word 'God' is that when it's used it's used as though we know what we're talking about."[21] For the anonymous author of *The Cloud of Unknowing*, God, or this place you come from, can never be fully known. It can only be an experience of unknowing. Thus, the purpose of engaging in meditative prayer is never to try and figure out *what* I am or *what* God is but rather to be conscious *that* I am and *that* God is.[22]

Devotion

I spoke with Cynthia Bourgeault about the differences between Centering Prayer and classical mindfulness practices. She shared that in her work with people from many contemplative traditions, she observes that the practices that carry people to a deeper commit-ment and embodiment of compassion are those that are "discretely, but clearly, rooted in a devotional tradition ... and I'm coming to suspect that the reason that's so, is because those deeper values are

20. Bourgeault, *The Heart of Centering Prayer*, 27.

21. John Phillip Newell, presentation, isle of Iona, Scotland, September 17, 2019.

22. Johnston, *The Cloud of Unknowing*, 8.

not carried in the mindfulness. *They're carried in the devotion.*"[23] Her words confirm suspicions I have raised that mindfulness can either serve self or society, depending on what values one brings to the practice. Bourgeault writes,

> Centering Prayer's unusual methodology makes complete sense only within a Christian theological frame of reference.... It was 10 years into my practice before I realized that the theological basis for Centering Prayer lies in the principle of kenosis, Jesus's self-emptying love that forms the core of his own self-understanding and life practice.[24]

The gentle release and letting go of thoughts is demonstrated, practiced, and learned through the technique of the prayer itself. Each time you notice a thought, which would include awareness of a breath, bodily sensation, sound, or emotion, you gently release your attention to it and return to the word you have chosen, to simple resting in a kind of pure awareness.

I have sat in meditation groups where Buddhists, Christians, and other practitioners sit together in silence. If you by chance walked by the lounge at the Congregational United Church of Christ every Wednesday morning in Pullman, Washington, some years ago where a group of religious leaders gathered weekly or by a chapel at Chapman University more recently where a group of faculty gathered early each Tuesday morning, you would never have known that the individuals sitting in a circle in silence were engaged in practices distinct from one another. The difference, I believe, is not as much in the actual practice itself—whether using a word or breath, you keep coming back to the present. But you may conceptualize the experience differently. For Christians, the experience of sitting in the present is one of sitting in Presence, the Presence of the Divine. This is a process of transformation in light of the resurrection, toward greater

---

23. Bourgeault, interview.
24. Bourgeault, *The Heart of Centering Prayer*, 33.

transparency to the movement of the Spirit within and through you. For Buddhism, mindfulness is understood in relation to the concept of nirvana, or freedom from suffering through liberation of the mind.

As can be imagined, Centering Prayer is not just an experience of bliss. Each time a person notices they are thinking, what they are observing may be thoughts that cause anguish and suffering. They may even be the result of resurfaced trauma. Recall my students coming to me with mixed and sometimes disturbing experiences after meditating. Father Keating describes Centering Prayer as something like divine psychotherapy during which one uncovers, layer by layer, those things that are inauthentic in one's life and actions. This experience of peeling back layers can even lead to a deep sense of abandonment. Keating describes this time as the "night of spirit."[25] The night of spirit is a time when all felt experience of the presence of God disappears. For Keating, this is a process of breaking down the ego self.

This night of spirit can be part of the process of shedding self-centeredness, the ego, and a false notion of the self. For St. John of the Cross, it is the "dark night of the soul" that affords this opportunity. He describes the dark night as one that involved, for him, a cleansing and purification of the soul, releasing abounding blessings.[26] Through a complete surrender and letting go of the self, a person comes to a renewed sense of being that is transformed into union with divine love.

Transparency

Perhaps the most profound aspect of Centering Prayer is the understanding that it is not we who are praying but the Spirit through us. We saw this expressed by Pastor Ben, when he articulated that if he accepts what comes to him, it goes through him. Father Keating

---

25. Thomas Keating, *Invitation to Love: The Way of Christian Contemplation* (New York: Continuum, 2003), chapter 15.

26. St. John of the Cross, *Dark Night of the Soul* (trans. E. Allison Peers; Mineola, NY: Dover Publications, 2012), 66, Kindle.

writes that in any prayer, we believe the presence of the Spirit is with and in us, inspiring and surrounding us as the unfolding of new life in Christ within and around us. In contemplative prayer, our own will and thoughts or reflections are bypassed, in a sense. "In other words, the Spirit prays in us and we consent."[27]

A contemporary of the author of The *Cloud of Unknowing*, Julian of Norwich, lived much of her life as a recluse in a cell built onto a church in Norwich, England. Travelers would arrive at her window daily to tell her of their troubles and receive her advice. Through her own experiences of illness and bliss, she describes God as personal and a great mystery at the same time, both immanent and transcendent. She writes of an experience of pure presence in which the boundaries between self and God disappear, where a person and God are knitted together. She calls this "Oneing," or becoming One with God.[28]

A Story of "Oneing"

After returning from Hawaii, I traveled to Moscow, Idaho, to see my friend Sharon Kehoe, who had recently been placed on hospice. Sharon was an accomplished scholar of religion, like her husband, Rob Snyder. They had recently returned from Corfu, where they had been living, so she could undergo cancer treatments.

The first time I met Father Keating, I was with Sharon. She taught religious studies and was director of the Campus Christian Center at the University of Idaho in Moscow. I was teaching as well, serving as director of the Common Ministry at Washington State University in Pullman, just seven miles over the state border. Some of the first women to do this work, we bonded through our love for campus ministry, our struggles in being taken seriously as women and thinking we had to work much harder than our male predecessors, and the decline in financial support for this work in the early twenty-first century.

---

27. Keating, *Open Mind*, 13.
28. Julian of Norwich, *Revelations of Divine Love* (trans. Grace Warrack; St. Paul, MN: Wilder Publications, 2011), 143, Kindle.

Sharon and I traveled together to the Garrison Institute symposium I described earlier in this book. During that week, we learned Centering Prayer from Father Keating, as well as contemplative rituals and meditations from Buddhist, Sufi, and Jewish teachers. After the conference ended, I began to realize that we had entered a deeper experience of presence after sitting in meditation together that week. For instance, I had a major annual auction to prepare for at my campus ministry when I returned home, and I did so without the usual panic and drama. I was in a "blissful" state of equanimity for about three weeks, where nothing that would normally bother me seemed of consequence. One morning, I awoke and felt a heaviness I immediately recognized as an initial stage of depression. I dragged myself out of bed because I had promised my friend Carolea Webb I would meet her for a walk.

As we traversed the former railroad bed surrounded by beautiful wheat-covered hills, our path lined with early spring flowers peering out among wispy weeds, I explained the heaviness I felt to Carolea. "What just happened?" I asked her. A long-time practicing Tibetan Buddhist, her answer surprised me. She affirmed that she had noticed a difference in me over the past weeks. "It's simple," she said, "you were in the Pureland." "The what?" I asked. "Christianity has no term for that! And why did I have to crash out of it?"

"The Pureland" is what meditation teachers sometimes refer to as a state of quiet and equanimity where your emotions are not bouncing around from the usual mental triggers that cause defensiveness and frustration. Sharon would laugh and say she was often in a state of unawareness of what was around her because she was caught up in the moment, but this was much more pronounced. I found myself hooked on meditation again, having practiced it sporadically but with little regularity since college—for probably all the wrong reasons. I wanted this blissful experience again. But in the ensuing years as I took Father Keating's advice to practice Centering Prayer twice a day for six months and never stop, I learned from meditation and from Sharon that Centering Prayer and meditation are not about bliss. They are about supporting you through the fullness of life as you live through both the pleasant and the unpleasant.

When I came to see Sharon in the beginning of what would indeed turn out to be the last six months of her life, she talked about the experience of being present. She referred to it as that experience when you say, "My gosh, I spent the whole afternoon talking like this, I had to be somewhere at four o'clock." For Sharon, it was an experience of the altering of space and time. She said, "Once you get to . . . 'the now,' we're sitting right here in the now intensely feeling this. Or we could feel it quietly, but it's (really) about the space between us, which is no longer between us, because now it's connecting us. So, space and time disappear."[29] All of time was like that for her as she drew close to the end of her life. She described it as getting to the experience of pure "presence."

For Sharon, this meant more than just getting lost in the moment. She described it, as did Julian of Norwich, as "Oneing" with the Divine and with another person. This goes beyond offering kindness to one another. Sharon called it an experience "where one person is all people and all people are one." As I sat with Sharon and Rob, hearing her words and experiencing this altering of time and space, I felt in the presence of divinity. Sharon's words closely echo Julian of Norwich's notion that one person is all people, and that all people are one person, in the sight of God.[30]

You might think that Sharon's life was filled with mental anguish once she learned there were no further cancer treatments that could save her life. Of course, it was devastating news. Yet she lived those final months completely in the present—whether it was pleasant or unpleasant. "It's like you're given a deadline," she said. "We always want to be in the present," she said, yet at the end of her life it was all she could do, so it truly happened. She wanted to spend her time

---

29. Sharon Kehoe and Rob Snyder, conversation with author, Moscow, ID (August 13, 2019).

30. Julian of Norwich, *Revelations of Divine Love*, 117.

"making meaning," talking with those who were meaningful to her, and being with her beloved. And that is just what she did.[31]

Centering Prayer and mindfulness both have the potential to open the heart of awareness, and Centering Prayer adds an ethical and spiritual foundation to the practice through devotion, intention, and transparency to the Divine. As Sharon's experience shows us, this orientation turns out to be the experience of Oneing, an immersion in love itself.

In addition to Centering Prayer, there is another practice in Christianity that is centered in love and unmistakably grounded in the ethics of dismantling social injustice. It is the long tradition of civil rights activism and acting on the side of the marginalized in any society. It has been characterized as a form of contemplative practice, where you are grounded in the *place you come from*—acting as the hands and feet of the Divine in the world. We turn to this practice next.

31. Kehoe and Snyder, conversation.

CHAPTER 10

Is Christianity Inconvenient to Empire?

Reliance on the Spirit produces not only a praise that is fervent, or a reliance on God that is ultimate, but also a commitment to a mission and ministry of life struggling against oppression, fighting for the poor, and seeking relief and justice for the weak.[1]

"Is it inconvenient to empire?"[2] Celtic scholar John Philip Newell posed this question as we sat in the St. Columba Hotel conference room on Scotland's isle of Iona. A wide berth of windows revealed sheep and highland cattle grazing in the pasture between us and the white-capped sea. Hilltops on the isle of Mull were visible in the distance, separating us from the mainland of Scotland. I gazed out on the expansive view while pondering his query in my mind: Is my action, is our action inconvenient to empire? By "empire" I understood him to mean regimes and governments that have been built on the backs of marginalized peoples, benefiting those in power while the majority live in impoverished conditions. Empire may also mean power amassed by a corporation or based on an ideology of racial or gendered superiority. For early Christians in the Celtic tradition, resistance to tyrannical rule was the true test of whether one's moti-

---

1. William J. Barber II, Liz Theoharis, and Rick Lowery, *Revive Us Again: Vision and Action in Moral Organizing* (Boston: Beacon Press, 2018), 24.

2. J. Philip Newell, presentation, Isle of Iona, September 16, 2019.

vation was authentic as a follower of Jesus. In this early Christian tradition, if one was devoted to transparency and justice and rooted in meditative practice, the call to act in ways inconvenient to human empire was central. Newell believes it to be at the heart of the Christian journey today, just as it was for early Celtic Christianity.

Each morning throughout my week on the isle of Iona, where natural landmarks, history, and legends abound of early Celtic spiritual roots, a community of travelers silently emerged from their rooms shortly after dawn. Each would walk in silence through the frosty morning air and cool ocean wind to Michael Chapel, nestled next to the more massive Iona Abbey. The small stone chapel dates to the thirteenth century. It rests between the abbey and the sea, and a peek inside reveals a simple, brown stone and wood sanctuary with a vaulted ceiling. We filed into the chapel in silence to sit on cold benches and hear the first utterance of the Michael Chapel Silent Prayer, and then began our thirty-minute time in silence. At the sound of the bell, these words were spoken and quiet ensued, ending only with another sounding of the bell and a chant.

Michael Chapel Silent Prayer

O Hidden Light,
Sun behind all suns,
Soul within all souls,
True life of every life,
This new day we give thee greeting.

Words from Scripture to lead us into silence:
"Be still and know that I am God."

All around us in the great cathedral of earth, sea, and sky,
Here among us in this ancient chapel of prayer,
And deep within us in the inner sanctuary of our being,
Let us be still and know.

Silence

Closing Chant
Om, Shalom, Ameen.[3]

Notice the creation emphasis of this prayer, on sun, life, earth, sea, sky, and inner being. In this ethos, God is revealed in every aspect of natural creation. It is an intimate understanding of the interconnectedness of everything, where God is closer to you than your very breath. Celtic mysticism holds that God is found in the light within each person and deep within the life of all of creation. The essence of Christian spirituality, inspired by this early tradition, is to dive headfirst into the world and its suffering, where you find God at the heart of suffering. Inspired by the apostle John, who was said to lean close enough against Jesus at the Last Supper to hear his heartbeat, Celtic understanding centers on listening to the heartbeat of God, which lends itself to "listening for God at the heart of life."[4]

The Celtic spiritual tradition characterized the young British church as early as the fourth century. Christianity was not yet mired in hierarchical theologies cemented by the Roman Catholic establishment or by the strict Calvinism that would be established later by Protestants in Edinburgh and across northern Europe. But by the end of and beyond the sixth century, Celtic Christianity was pushed to the fringes, at times violently, by the institutionalized church. The latter emphasized hearing God's word through the church, while Celtic Christianity followed the long tradition of listening for the heartbeat of God in and caring for all of creation.[5]

Back on the mainland of Scotland I spoke with Ali Newell, associate chaplain at the University of Edinburgh, who has been instrumental in bringing mindfulness to the university. She finds it is extremely

---

3. J. Philip Newell, used by permission from author.
4. J. Philip Newell, *Listening for the Heartbeat of God* (New York: Paulist Press, 1997), 2.
5. Newell, *Listening for the Heartbeat,* 2–3.

useful for the community. Yet, she told me when I visited her office on the university campus that she observes how easily the practice of mindfulness can get stuck on a focus on the individual. "It's the experience of love and compassion and going deeper and finding the center" she is interested in.[6] And she finds that experience in the Celtic spiritual approach, which says that within every person is a light—the light of God. But it doesn't even stop there. It insists that the task of each person is to see the light in others. Every other person. All other people. People even from faiths different from your own.

She marvels at how revolutionary this is. "There are people that talk about . . . a light within every person." But the Celtic tradition, she emphasizes, goes further, saying that "you *expect to find that* in each person. That's a very different approach!"[7]

Seeing the light within each person is possible when you give way to seeing as the Spirit would. Listening from the heart is akin to answering a call from God. The call of the heart has been described as becoming a new person with a social conscience. This is the call of a heart of compassion, capable of hearing the cry of those suffering and capable of responding.[8] The language of a "call" toward faithfulness to a gospel that sides with the oppressed is built into the foundations and a prophetic tradition throughout Christian history.

Although central here, this is not a concept confined to Christianity. In the directors of our chapel staff at the Fish Interfaith Center at Chapman University, who are Black, white, of Asian descent, gay, straight, Muslim, Christian, Jewish, and Hindu, I see their shared understanding that acting on behalf of the marginalized of society is not just a matter of politics or personal choice but a responsibility they are all called to. I witness each of them doing the work of compassion with gratefulness, as a response to that inner calling.

---

6. Ali Newell, interview with author, University of Edinburgh, September 25, 2019.

7. Newell, interview.

8. John Neafsey, *A Sacred Voice Is Calling: Personal Vocation and Social Conscience* (Maryknoll, NY: Orbis Books, 2006), loc. 95 of 3267, Kindle.

Measuring one's Christian practice by asking whether it is inconvenient to empire or whether it offers challenge to empires that oppress marginalized people unjustly has occured throughout other eras within Christianity. The message of Black and progressive white churches protesting the Vietnam War and calling for civil rights in the 1960s is one example. Barbara Holmes draws a clear parallel between contemplative practice, justice work, and the dismantling of empire building. In *Joy Unspeakable: Contemplative Practices of the Black Church*, Holmes writes,

> When the word contemplation comes to my mind, I think of Thomas Merton and his lengthy and illuminating discourses about the practices that include complete dependence on God.
>
> But I also want to talk about Martin Luther King Jr. and his combination of interiority and activism, Howard and Sue Bailey Thurman and their inward journeys. I want to present Sojourner Truth, Harriet Tubman, Fannie Lou Hamer, Barbara Jordan, and the unknown black congregations that sustained whole communities without fanfare or notice. Like Christianity, contemplative practices come in many forms; these practices have survived and thrived through inculturation and ethnic adaptation.[9]

Holmes finds in each of these practices an inner space of contemplation. This embodied locus of contemplation is aptly described by theologian and activist Howard Thurman's metaphor of an "inward sea" guarded by an angel, through whom nothing is able to pass unless it "has the mark of your inner authority." This inward sea is your critical link with the Eternal. Thurman refers to the importance of developing a "central stillness of spirit," and at times coming to a "point of rest, a place of pause."[10]

9. Barbara A. Holmes, *Joy Unspeakable: Contemplative Practices of the Black Church* (Minneapolis, MN: Fortress Press), 3–4, Kindle.

10. Howard Thurman, *Meditations of the Heart* (Boston, MA: Beacon Press, 1999), 16, 24, 29, Kindle.

Civil rights leaders within the Christian tradition have drawn on this inward sea of strength as a link with the Eternal as a primary motivator for engaging in social change. Yet the source of Christian civil rights leaders' motivation is easily misunderstood when persons of faith are invoked as examples within the contemporary mindfulness movement. Consider the following statement by a mindfulness expert: "Emotional resilience is crucial to any great social movement, allowing change-makers to mirror what they hope to bring to the world: peace, justice, equality, and relief from suffering." The author then invokes figures including Martin Luther King Jr. and Nelson Mandela and continues, "While these great leaders may draw their equanimity from their spiritual practice, secular mindfulness can provide similar benefits. It can help us empathize more deeply with others, notice their distress in our bodies, and thus feel compelled to act on their behalf."[11]

It is possible that one might be compelled to act on another's behalf in part because they have noticed distress in their own body, which motivates empathy with others. Yet it is preposterous to assume that what motivates these faith leaders to engage in nonviolent revolution challenging oppressive regimes is reducible to noticing the distress in their bodies.

Andrew Young has described the words and actions of Martin Luther King Jr., which infuse ultimate reality and our political, social existence, as "nothing less than the voice of God coming through the life of one of his young, humble, and obedient servants."[12] King himself described this call as a privilege for any whose loyalties run beyond the nation's goals when he spoke out against U.S. involvement in Vietnam. In his speech "Beyond Vietnam," he articulated the call

---

11. Erica Marcus, "Mindfulness: A Tool for Social Justice," *Wise Minds. Big Hearts*, September 23, 2015, http://www.wiseminds-bighearts.com.

12. Clayborne Carson and Kris Shepard, eds., *A Call to Conscience: The Landmark Speeches of Dr. Martin Luther King, Jr.* (New York: Grand Central Publishing, 2001), 38, Kindle.

to stand on the side of victims, enemies of the nation, and those who are weak or without voice.[13]

In contemporary times we hear this echoed in the voices of clergy, including Rev. Dr. William Barber II and Rev. Dr. Liz Theoharis, cofounders of the Poor People's Campaign. In the aftermath of the lynching of George Floyd on the streets of Minneapolis, as it was characterized by Barber, he said, "As a pastor, I turn to scripture in times of crisis. . . . Those of us who have faced the lethal force of systematic racism have also learned that we can be wounded healers."[14] Barber is also president and senior lecturer of Repairers of the Breach, which seeks to build a "moral movement" uplifting our deepest constitutional and moral values. The movement challenges any position claiming solely that the greatest moral issues facing the country are property rights, abortion, or prayer in public schools. Instead, it insists that the most pressing public concerns of our faith traditions are how our society treats the poor, women, LGBTQ people, children, workers, immigrants, communities of color, and the sick. Environmental, criminal, and economic justice are the movement's top priorities.[15] Repairers of the Breach powerfully places a "death measurement" on public policies and bills proposed by Congress, measuring what their impact will be—how many people, particularly Black people and poor people, will die if the policy is enacted.[16]

This work of dismantling the building of an empire that has been built on the backs of marginalized peoples, addressing issues like unjust wages and poverty, is central to liberation theology, a movement that began in the mid-twentieth century in Latin America.[17]

---

13. Martin Luther King Jr., "Beyond Vietnam," in Carson and Shepard, eds., *A Call to Conscience*, 145–46.

14. William J. Barber, II, "A Pastoral Letter to the Nation," May 31, 2020, www.breachrepairers.org.

15. "Higher Ground Moral Declaration," www.breachrepairers.org.

16. William J. Barber, II, "America, Accepting Death Is Not an Option Anymore," June 14, 2020, www.breachrepairers.org.

17. See the seminal work by Gustavo Gutiérrez, *A Theology of Liberation:*

But the ideas of this theology are not new to Christianity. Jesus himself was killed by the Roman Empire when he was called "Son of God," a title only used by Caesar, and when he championed the vast majority of people under tyrannical Roman rule who were at the time slaves or servants. Barber and Theoharis stand in a long line of Christian theologians who have drawn strength from their faith toward the dismantling of oppressive regimes.

Questioning "Surrender"

The Celtic tradition resisted empire, from early Roman times to confrontations with the early Scottish Protestant church. Jesus himself posed serious opposition to the Roman Empire, exercising a ministry that was deeply threatening to a Roman Empire maintained by force and control. Through words and actions, he ushered in a "revolution of compassion" to vast crowds of people and welcomed those who were outcasts and living in poverty.[18] Today, Barber and Theoharis lead a movement to dismantle the systematic injustice in which the contemporary church and society both participate. Yet we must acknowledge that Christianity has been hijacked by empires over and over. From violent Crusades wiping out entire populations unless they professed Christianity to the Holocaust to the practice of forcing young people from Native cultures into boarding schools and violently indoctrinating them into white Christian ideology—these are horrific blights on the soul of Christianity.

More recently, preachers of what we can characterize as the "prosperity gospel" amass enormous empires of wealth in the name of Jesus, whom they have completely sold out by abandoning any concern for the least among us. Political science professor John Compton suggests that today, this is in part because the authority of the clergy

---

History, Politics, Salvation (English trans., Maryknoll, NY: Orbis Books, 1973).

18. Gail J. Stearns, *Open Your Eyes: Toward Living More Deeply in the Present* (Eugene, OR: Wipf & Stock, 2011), 8.

in America has shifted dramatically. He notes that a major reason evangelical pastors are willing to abdicate even personal moral ethics for politics and thus to support a politician like President Trump—who cannot be characterized as behaving morally even by the most conservative evangelical standards—is that pastors have lost standing in general in the community. In order to fill their pews, white Protestants who once might have offered moral guidance and condemned structural injustice from the pulpit now take their cue from what people would like to hear.[19]

Throughout Christian history, theology has been twisted to benefit those in power. Concepts that are central to contemplation, like *surrender, self-sacrifice,* and *selflessness,* have been manipulated to maintain social control. White feminist theologians pointed out years ago that Church Fathers have long highlighted *pride* as one of the deadliest of sins as a way of keeping their own power. How convenient it is to teach this to those they oppress in order to encourage those with lowly status to take on even more humility through humiliation, thus cementing their oppression. In the 1970s, feminist theology found motivation toward justice for women through theological subversion of the notion of sin, suggesting that the greatest sin of those who are oppressed is more likely *lack* of pride.[20]

Since then, theologians from many more communities have carried this challenge to the Christian requirement of sacrifice much further. Womanist theologians emphasize that focusing on women's liberation from the patriarchy cannot be seen as entailing individual self-sacrifice; in fact, they insist, liberation is not an individual pursuit at all. Drawing from Alice Walker's definition, a "womanist" is "committed to survival and wholeness of entire people, male *and* female.

---

19. John W. Compton, *The End of Empathy: Why White Protestants Stopped Loving Their Neighbors* (New York: Oxford University Press, 2020).

20. Valerie Saiving, "The Human Situation: A Feminine View," in Carol P. Christ and Judith Plaskow, eds., *Womanspirit Rising: A Feminist Reader in Religion* (San Francisco: Harper & Row, 1979), 25–42.

Not a separatist, except periodically, for health."[21] Liberation must be sought both for individual bodies and for the whole people if it is to be liberation at all. Sin itself is redefined as communal. Oppression occurs through systematic, structural violence, not just through the transgressions of individuals alone.[22]

The idea of selflessness, which has functioned throughout Christian history as a justification for violence against the marginalized, has been reclaimed and celebrated as a resistance strategy against oppression. The church has manipulated devotion to Jesus's mother, Mary, for example, as a revered sacrificial mother in order to justify and further perpetuate female subservience. Yet, as Chung Hyun Kyung notes, Mary choosing to give birth as a single mother when such a position was dangerous, and later supporting her son in solidarity with his movement, offers empowerment for Asian women.[23] Mary standing in a community of women who refuse to run away from the brutal political murder of her son models resistance to state violence. This stance has been repeated by such communal movements as the Argentinian *Madres de Plaza de Mayo*, which mobilizes the image of Mary against oppressive political regimes that have abducted and killed thousands of the children of mothers in this movement.[24]

---

21. Alice Walker, "Womanist," in Alice Walker, *In Search of Our Mothers' Gardens: Womanist Prose* (Orlando, FL: Harcourt Brace Jovanovich, 1983), xi–xii.

22. For recent and earlier womanist theology, see Pamela R. Lightsey, *Our Lives Matter: A Womanist Queer Theology* (Eugene, OR: Pickwick Publications, 2015); and Delores Williams, *Sisters in the Wilderness: The Challenge of Womanist God-Talk* (Maryknoll, NY: Orbis Books, 1993).

23. Chung Hyun Kyung, *Struggle to Be the Sun Again: Introducing Asian Women's Theology* (Maryknoll, NY: Orbis Books, 1990), chapter 5.

24. Kathleen Elkins Gallagher, *Mary, Mother of Martyrs: How Motherhood Became Self-Sacrifice in Early Christianity* (Eugene, OR: Wipf & Stock, 2020), 25–28.

Contemplative Practice for the Dismantling of Empire

Many Christian communities discern their call as combining social justice and contemplative practice. Here are just a couple of the examples I have encountered.

The Brothers of Taizé

At any given time, dozens of the Brothers of Taizé, themselves hailing from multiple countries, are scattered across the continents serving the poor. When in residence at Taizé, they teach and serve young people who arrive from around the world by the thousands to live in simplicity, assist in daily chores, and share together three times a day prayer, song, and silence. The setting is idyllic, surrounded by green pastures in the hills of the Burgundy region of France. Throughout much of the year, young people come for a week at a time, staying in rustic bunkhouses or camping outdoors. Very simple communal meals are eaten sitting on benches outside the church and minimal buildings, as they join in a space and pace of simplicity and reverence.

On a visit to Taizé, I entered La Morada, a building that houses offices for the brothers. While I waited, I spoke at length with Bartosz, a young volunteer. He had come for what he thought would be a few weeks, a year ago. Bartosz said that when he came to Taizé, he felt he had lost his purpose and lost his way. He thought he would soon be leaving. But he said that the brothers just welcome you, as do the prayers, which are powerful and peaceful. He attends them daily, along with managing volunteer jobs the brothers have assigned to him.[25]

Brother Stephen soon arrived, and we retired to the back of the building and found two folding chairs under a shade tree where we could sit for several hours away from the crowds. He told me that the core of Taizé has always been something they call "struggle and contemplation," by which they mean that "prayer without social action is

---

25. Bartosz, interview with author, Taizé, France, September 10, 2019.

nothing." He clarified, "Well, almost nothing!"[26] He said the brothers were living quietly, sharing prayer in a quaint church in Taizé, when in the 1960s people started arriving. He believes they liked the prayers and simplicity and discovered that the brothers listened to them during a tumultuous time, including Vietnam and growing movements for animal rights and women's rights. Soon there were hundreds of young visitors coming daily. He explained:

> There was a meeting at the beginning, and some of the brothers said, "We have to close. We have to tell them they can't come here." And then an older brother said, "If they're coming here, it must be God who's sending them. And, in that case, then it's our responsibility to welcome them in." ... It's a remarkable thing to adapt and figure out a way to do that with different languages, and make it simple, and not just say, "We don't want these people," or, "What are they doing?"[27]

The Brothers of Taizé now have friends all over the world. Brother Stephen said he notices that they do something that may be unusual. Everywhere they go, the brothers have their ears open to the news. It is part of the prayers to hold up those suffering in particular places and circumstances across the world each day.

The Sisters of St. Gertrude

For many years, I took solo retreats and brought students for retreat to St. Gertrude's Monastery in Cottonwood, Idaho. Set in the beautiful hills just east of the Salmon River as it snakes its way through central Idaho along the Rocky Mountains, the Sisters of St. Gertrude are known throughout the region for their reforestation of the hills. The sisters are made up of health-care professionals, teachers, writers, artists and craftspersons, pastoral care providers, retreat directors,

---

26. Brother Stephen Braithwaite, interview with author, Taizé, France, September 10, 2019.

27. Braithwaite, interview.

and more. Three times daily I would enter the beautiful stone chapel to join the sisters for prayers and responsive readings of the Psalms, and sometimes readings from a commentary on the *Rule of Benedict* by Joan Chittister.[28] Every responsive reading from the Psalms caught me up short at first because of the very slow cadence. I quickly realized I needed to slow my breathing into a meditative pattern to repeat each line along with the sisters. Silence hung between each phrase, with reflective pauses throughout.

On one visit to the monastery, I entered the dining room to meet Sister Mary Kay, then prioress of St. Gertrude's. Curious about the reading of the Psalms and prayers the sisters gathered for three times a day, I had asked to speak with her. As we sat with a cup of coffee at a dining table, I had just one question. I asked her to tell me about prayer.

Sister Mary Kay explained to me that prayer is God's act; it is not something we do. She went on to clarify that if you get serious about prayer, three things will happen. First, you will come to face yourself in a new way. Second, you will find yourself changing, and giving up things you have been holding onto. And finally, if you truly get serious about prayer, you will have to do the works of justice.[29]

This remarkable response reminds me of the claim of mindfulness that it may change you, and the claim of Centering Prayer that you will have to give things up. But Sister Mary Kay's claim that you will have no choice, that *you will have to do the works of justice*, rings true for those who combine the interiority and activism of Christianity.

How do you discern the call of the heart? For Christians who pay attention to an inner voice of the Spirit while also staying attentive to the news revealing suffering in the world, the call of the heart is heard through the stillness of silent prayer.

---

28. Joan Chittister, OSB, *The Rule of Benedict: Insights for the Ages* (New York: Crossroad Publishing, 2004).

29. I originally told this story in Stearns, *Open Your Eyes*, 29–30.

Mindfulness and Christian Practice

Within the framework of Christianity are ancient contemplative practices including Centering Prayer, where prayer and meditation move one to do the works of justice, as Sister Mary Kay espouses. Coupled with the urge for economic, political, and social justice at the heart of the message of Jesus, Christianity brings a moral framework for awakening to injustice today. It offers agency for deep change in the world. Combining the accessible tools of mindfulness with Christian contemplative prayer can offer a practice for awakening to the present and our capacity to bring about change in the world.

Here are three meditative practices to begin bringing practical mindfulness tools to our commitment to awaken to ourselves, our compassion for others, and even to the expansive presence of God. The first is a *relational* meditation, training ourselves to be fully present with another person. You may find that this practice can be carried over to listening to a group, a speaker, or even a crowd. It is a way to set our own agenda aside and really listen.

When you are talking with a person, whether they have come to you for advice or just to talk or you encountered them for some other reason, practice what it means to simply listen, without any agenda. This exercise is not helpful when someone is speaking to you in a way that is minimizing or harming you or is exercising a position of authority over you. Choose a time you are not in a vulnerable situation and feel a sense of safety and trust. I find that sometimes when I do this meditation, as I listen, the awareness of space and time around me begins to drop away and I am *only* listening. You may find that when it is your turn to respond, it does not come rapidly, but with more accuracy than you might have responded with otherwise. Or perhaps listening was enough, and no response is necessary. You can practice this with a friend or two. Set a timer for two to five minutes per person, and ask one person at a time to answer a prompt or talk about something that is on their mind, while the others simply listen.

Listening Meditation Exercise

- As you listen, consciously open awareness to your breath, and ground yourself in this space, this time, this breath.
- Listen to the sound of the speaker's voice as you would listen to sounds around you, allowing each word, thought, phrase, and meaning to enter your hearing as it occurs.
- Notice emotions that may arise. If they are too intense, allow yourself to take a break, find a way to exit the conversation, or bring your attention into your own breath and body. If they are simply emotions you notice and can be curious about, allow yourself that awareness, then reground in your breath and continue listening.
- You may become aware that you are thinking of something else or beginning to form your response and have ceased to listen. See if you can let that go as well, ground in your breath, and listen to what you are hearing at this moment.

A second meditation is a *walking* meditation, and it can be especially effective if one is able to walk outside (though it can be adapted for people who are seated or are inside). Here is how a walking meditation went for me this morning when I took my dog for a meandering stroll through the park adjacent to my home. I consciously grounded myself in the sensations of my feet touching the ground and repeated my sacred word. I then allowed the word to drop away and noted what I saw or sensed: *green grass, litter, blue sky, cool breeze, unhoused or homeless man, playground, father, son, love.*

Next, I shifted my labeling, so that what appeared turned into *my idea of grass, my idea of litter, my idea of blue sky, my idea of cool breeze, my idea of homeless man*, and so on. I then went further to notice my reactions: *my dislike of seeing litter, my feeling of contentment from cool breeze*, etc.

You can shift from labeling *car*, for example, to *my idea of car* during one walking session, or just name *car* a number of practice days in a row, then shift to *my idea of car*, and eventually to *my aversion to car* for some days in a row. You will become aware of likes and dislikes or of things that minimize or expand your consciousness. At some point, you may find that what appears elicits an expanded sensation of *awe*, as happened to me upon seeing a father tenderly helping his son on the playground. You might then name what you experience, such as *awe*, *love*, or *God*. In discussing this meditation, Jim Burklo notes that you may begin to notice that your observation and experience is based not on the real essence of things but on your idea of them. He affirms, "When you are awake to the possibility that the world around you has an essence that is beyond your ideas and opinions, you have awakened to God." You may begin to glimpse all you see and hear encompassed in an expanded experience of Presence, of God.[30]

Walking Naming/Unnaming Meditation

1. Take a walk outside or be outside as you are able. Begin by repeating your word, and as you do so and if you are walking, feel the movement of your feet on the ground. If sitting or inside, begin repeating your word to the cadence of your breath.

2. As you look around begin naming what you see or hear. For example: *tree, loud car, dog, breeze,* etc. If something that appears elicits a feeling of dislike or like, just notice. You may even sense an expansion of your heart, and an experience of awe, which you can name as *awe, God, love,* etc.

3. Next, shift your perspective, and as you see or hear something new, say to yourself as it appears: *my idea of tree, my idea of loud car, my idea of awe,* etc.

4. Next, notice your emotions and thoughts, and name these as well: *my opinion of liking that tree, my aversion to loud car, my feeling of expansion with awe,* etc.

---

30. See Jim Burklo, *Mindful Christianity* (Haworth, NJ: St. Johann Press, 2017), 13–14. "Naming/Unnaming Meditation," adapted with permission from Burklo.

5. You may find yourself expanding consciousness to notice things with less judgment and vaster awareness, even seeing God in all things.

A third meditation is a *sound* meditation. When I moved into the townhouse I currently live in, the one hesitation I had was that it borders a busy street. Throughout the day I hear constant traffic. I became used to wearing noise-canceling earbuds for meditation, but I gradually found I used them less and less. I recall a teacher once commenting at a retreat that you can become fully awakened just by listening to traffic come and go! And when I mentioned this dislike of traffic sounds to my friend Beth Shields, she simply told me, "That is your ocean." Standing at the ocean brings the soothing repetition of sound, naturally coming and going with the waves. And looking out at the vast ocean brings awareness of the vastness of our planet. In one moment, we can feel small and at the same time interconnected with all that is. This simple meditation helps us to gain that awareness every day. We feel humble before God and yet a part of God and all of creation.

With this sound meditation, you might practice just the noting of sounds for a number of days in a row. Begin with five minutes, as it is comfortable for you, and add a few more minutes each day until you reach twenty. Then you may feel ready to move onto allowing your awareness to expand beyond the sound as far as your consciousness reaches, and rest there for another five to ten minutes.

Sound Meditation
1. Sit in a comfortable position and close your eyes. Begin your meditation by repeating your sacred word as you inhale and exhale. Notice any sensations that appear.
2. Gradually open your hearing sense door, becoming aware of sounds as they appear. Just relax, allowing your mind to rest, repeating your word as long as you find it helpful. It will likely drop away at some point, which is natural.

3. Allow your attention to flow. As a sound appears notice and follow it; when it is no longer audible, notice what is here now. It may be another sound, or silence. See if you can stay with whatever is appearing. (You may find you are analyzing or naming the sounds and even getting caught in a story about them. Allow each thought to fade just as sounds do, aware of what is here now.)

4. When you are ready, stretch your hearing as far as it can go. What is the farthest sound or vibration you can hear? Children like to imagine they have superpowers like those of a favorite superhero. How far does your hearing, your awareness, expand?

5. As you notice the almost unlimited expansion of your consciousness, beyond hearing, you may begin to awaken to the limitlessness of consciousness, the Eternal.

Reverend Dr. William Barber argues that the followers of Jesus and the early church included throngs of people who depended on one another. They were committed to prosperity. But that prosperity did not come about through self-focused acts or through individual greed or accumulation of wealth. It included prosperity for the entire community.[31] Some questions must be asked today: Is Christianity challenging systematic injustice? If not, is it not true to Jesus himself? A primary purpose for Jesus's life was to usher in a realm of God on earth characterized by a revolution of compassion for the least of those among us. According to the writers of the Gospels, particularly the Gospel of Mark, Jesus often went away and called his disciples to do the same, to rest and pray. They drew energy, developed in quiet contemplation, for a life of service to any and all. Jesus healed and taught persons whether they were of his ethnicity or not, his religion or not, his class standing or not.[32]

31. Barber et al., *Revive Us Again*, 13.
32. Stearns, *Open Your Eyes*, 8–11.

John Philip Newell sees much that is positive in the mindfulness movement and suggests that one way we can evaluate a movement's efficacy is to ask whether it is bringing about compassion. As we find new ways to integrate mindfulness tools into our spiritual practices of prayer and meditation, the test of authenticity is whether we can answer that question in the affirmative. When we look at our practice, Newell suggests we might ask, "Is it releasing compassionate action? Is it releasing interrelations?" In other words, is our practice purposefully moving us to compassion, and is it helping us to build relations between ourselves and others toward the work of justice?[33]

---

33. J. Philip Newell, interview.

Conclusion

In *Conjuring Freedom*, Johari Jabir demonstrates the remarkable way Black regiments during the Civil War converted tools of domination that were designed to assimilate them into a racist, exploitive society into organized but unrecognized protest. Summoning spiritual power, they transformed tools of sound and song into new forms of masculinity, solidarity, and dignity that promoted change in society. But Jabir cautions:

> Sometimes in attempting to fool their oppressors, however, members of aggrieved groups can fool themselves. Tools that seem like infinitely malleable and ideologically neutral technologies can instead be so structured in dominance that they reinforce rather than resist dominant ways of knowing and being.[1]

I have argued that the use of mindfulness tools can pose a similar danger. Caught up as we are in societal constructions of *happiness* and adopting the language of *stressism*, we have wrapped mindfulness into a cloak serving a dominant, patriarchal, white-supremacist, and consumeristic empire.

We are being called today to turn around and see another point of view. If we stand upon a mountain and gaze in one direction, we see a landscape—that of the American mindfulness scene. But if we turn around and see the vast array of spiritual practices imbued with imperatives of liberation and love, including some that gave rise to

---

1. Johari Jabir, *Conjuring Freedom: Music and Masculinity in the Civil War's "Gospel Army"* (Columbus: Ohio State University Press, 2017), loc. 219 of 6646, Kindle.

the mindfulness movement itself, there is a completely new vision before us.

Womanist, feminist, and queer theorists analyzing sexist and racist oppression have long called for an entirely different perspective from that of patriarchal white supremacy. The heart of our culture is calling for this pivot today, motivated by stirrings of past and present pain and sparked by hopes of a liberated future. This is what I believe Jesus meant by telling his followers to "repent"—to turn around and embrace a completely new vision of how to act in the world. As we slowly pivot, mindfulness is revealed as a cultural construction benefitting some (to the tune of billions of dollars each year) but leaving many behind, living with unchallenged social, economic, and structural systems of injustice that cause enormous difficulty for those least entitled by the systems. We rotate our view and begin to envision a new way of being, one that is faithful, ethical, and dedicated to collective resistance and transformation.

If we believe mindfulness tools have greater potential than just bringing about personal enhancement, we need to couple them with ethical intention and with gratefulness for life and the lives of those who are not usually encompassed within the lives that "matter" in society. Just as Buddhist teachers begin a retreat encouraging students to adopt a set of moral precepts, we can encourage each person to determine their ethical context for mindfulness practice. If we are teachers, we might put a warning label on our upcoming courses, such as: this practice may open your world to the extent that you find morally you cannot continue the way you are currently living; it may engage your inner activist; it may bring up understandings of how just by being a part of this society you are participating in systematic injustice; and it may reveal just how deeply your life is shaped by sexism or racism.

In our courses and retreats and mindfulness groups, if we are white, we need to listen. When needed for the health of some participants, we need to support opportunities for separating based on gendered or racial identities with which our companions in mindfulness groups self-identify. If we are white, we need to do our own inner work and confer with our colleagues and students to unpack our participation in systems of racism. If we are male, we similarly need to unpack our cooperation with systems of sexism. We can defer to the people among us who don't just read the books on feminism or racism or study feminist theory or critical race theory but, having grown up experiencing and affected by systematic ways these forces operate in society, have also *lived* these realities. We can awaken to the language surrounding mindfulness that is used as rhetoric of power to keep people from connecting with one another and bringing about liberatory change. We can awaken to the language of culture that is designed to deny collaborative liberation by keeping us preoccupied with self-care alone, blind to our participation in wider practices of bias.

If we are practicing mindfulness solely to find relief from stresses or pain in our daily lives, so be it; but let us be aware that that is what we are doing. Then we can't claim that by doing this practice alone we will change the world. We'll just lessen our daily stress or pain, and that is no small matter. If we are practicing because the company we work for has determined it will help us become a more productive employee, then we need to be up front with ourselves about both the employer's and our own intentions for practice. It may be just another company program required for you to accept your tasks without complaint and do your job better so production will increase.

If we are doing mindfulness in order to gain equanimity in difficult circumstances, wonderful. Then we might seek to go even deeper than listening to an app a day and move toward long-term commitment. We may have the courage to shift our patterns of thinking and our entire orientation to the world of which we are a tiny part, including examining our ethics and values in relationship to that world.

In her baccalaureate speech to the Chapman University graduating students, Valarie Kaur acknowledged that the diploma each of them was receiving that weekend would make their dreams of being a lawyer or an artist or a businessperson possible. She went on,

But you will be sorely tempted to use that diploma instead to hide from the fires of this world. That is the temptation of privilege. Your diploma which should open you to the world can be used to blind you to everything except your own safety, your own comfort, your own celebrity, your own status, your own happiness. And here's the thing, society will not judge you harshly for it. No, society will exalt you for it. And yet, that is my greatest fear for you.[2]

This is the fear that has come true today in the mindfulness movement: a practice that has the capacity to open us to the world is being used to blind us to our privilege (in those of us who are privileged), and to steer us toward our own, individual pursuit of happiness as defined by society. And our cooperation in the more deceptive intentions of this movement is benefiting many by supporting a billion-dollar mindfulness industry.

It is time to stop being afraid to allow others—or ourselves—to be immersed in the language, ritual, meditation, prayer, and music of our ancestors and communities for deeper context in which to integrate mindfulness tools.

We can start by examining and eliminating the fear that coupling mindfulness tools with communal ethical or spiritual or religious theologies and practices somehow taints mindfulness. Instead, we see that paired with these, mindfulness becomes a tool for resisting injustices that are embedded within dominant culture. The coupling of ethics, compassion, and service is embedded within and being lived out today through communities of faith and spiritual practice.

Equally, we can see that we have a unique opportunity to open up a new set of tools that will enable the foundation of compassion within our faith traditions to spring forth anew. Mindfulness tools are some of the most accessible, effective methods today to awaken us to our own minds. We might even take the advice to practice twenty

---

2. Valarie Kaur, Chapman University Interfaith Baccalaureate Service Address, Orange, CA, May 20, 2016, https://www.chapman.edu/fic.

minutes, twice a day, in the context of our faith, with the promise that it may change our life. Just imagine if it caused us to face ourselves anew and to understand the divine in a completely revolutionary way, and even moved us to have to do the works of justice.

We can engage in gratefulness of heart. In each of the religious and spiritual traditions we have touched upon, giving thanks is central. It is found whether one engages in repetition of the Psalms, the *shabads*, the dharma, chants from African roots, or the poetry of the mystics. We are not just offering a debt of gratitude to something that is outside of or apart from ourselves. In contemplative understanding, gratefulness mystically flows through us. It also flows through us in actuality, to move us to action. I hold much gratefulness for the tools of mindfulness and for the deep and ancient practices that highlight compassion for creation and humanity, and for those who have the courage to bring them together.

I hope this journey has opened for you, as it has for me, the possibility for transformation. We have a tremendous opportunity to use mindfulness tools, steeped in our particular theologies of practice, for the purpose of liberation. The tools of mindfulness might not just be inconvenient to empire. They could be tools to help change the world.

One Final Story

Due to precautions during the COVID-19 pandemic, for a year and a half I wasn't able to see my mother, who was living with dementia. When I finally saw her, I realized that she may have forgotten I was her daughter, but that she knew I was family and someone special as soon as she looked up at me. I knew that because her face softened as she said, "Oh, my . . ." We hugged, after so many months apart, and our eyes filled with tears.

Nearing her ninety-fifth birthday, she was quite frail and lived in a continual state of physical pain. But she was still able, with help, to get up, dress, eat, and take part in some daily activities. Being with my mother could be challenging, as questions were repeated and conversations became circular. At one point I was across the room sorting through her papers and clothing and she said, "I want to ask you some questions." I came back and sat on the edge of her bed to listen and answer the same questions she had already asked, again. As my sister Nancy said, being with our mother in the final years of her life was the best practice in just being mindful.

I would not call having a mother with dementia something that brought me or my sisters, Jane and Nancy, any happiness as we shared caring for her. Nor would I call her life during those last years one filled with happiness, for a woman who once was loved by everyone who knew her, and was a capable, professional nursing instructor, mother, volunteer, and person of faith. She had an uncanny ability to be the first to show up, casserole in hand, and to network with the community to help ill or grieving people to receive any care they needed. Everything our culture calls and claims as happiness, including physical ability, independence, mental sharpness, and purpose, later eluded her.

The third day in a row that I had finally been able to be with Mom, I walked into her room in the evening just as she was crawling into bed. She sat up on the edge of the bed beside me and chatted. She was more animated than usual, talking of her mother and father and step-mother and childhood experiences. "How old am I?" she asked, looking straight at me with wide eyes, like a young girl perched on the edge of the bed eager to hear the answer. I told her she was ninety-four. She leaned closer toward me, looking directly into my eyes, and an impish smile appeared. "Truthfully," she grinned, "Truthfully, how old am I?" She knew she was joking, and she knew she could not recall, all at once. I left her that evening with my heart overflowing—not with happiness, for it brought my heart pain to see her this way, but with pure love.

In one of her more lucid moments earlier that day, Mom had commented on how hard it was for her to remember things anymore. "Why does God do this?" she asked. I started to say I didn't know, when, to my surprise, she answered her own question: "Maybe God just wants us to take care of each other."

Circling back to that elusive concept of truth, we see that liberating mindfulness means utilizing mindfulness tools to loosen the grip of stress on us while opening our eyes to the true causes of our shared stresses. Many of those are due to structural, historic injustices embedded in our culture, politics, and economics. They are not inevitable and can only be alleviated if we wake up, together. Other stresses do not need to be eliminated, like some natural processes of aging; yet the burden of difficulty is disproportionately visited on those without resources or access to health or elder care, finances, nutrition, or shelter. They could instead be understood for what they are—communal difficulties, which we bear together. May we finally resist and awaken. May we finally really care for one another.

Index